The reconstituted family

The reconstituted family:
a study of remarried couples and their children

Lucile Duberman

Nelson-Hall Publishers · Chicago

Library of Congress Cataloging in Publication Data

Duberman, Lucile, 1926-
   The reconstituted family.

   Bibliography: p.
   Includes index.
   1.   Remarriage—United States.   2.   Family—U-
nited States.   3.   Stepchildren—United States.
I.   Title.
HQ536.D82   301.42'7   75-8840
ISBN 0-88229-168-8

Manufactured in the United States of America.

With love to my
husband, Ralph Kaminsky

Contents

List of tables

TABLES

Preface

This study of remarried men and women who have children from previous marriages arose out of personal interest and experience. In 1956 my first husband and I were divorced. In 1960 I married a man who had four children. His two oldest children were boys aged fourteen and twelve; his daughters were ten and nine. My own children at the time of the remarriage were aged sixteen, thirteen, and nine.

My second husband and I retained custody of my three children and his two sons. We bought a large, old house in the suburbs of New York City and proceeded to become a "family." To this end, my husband and I enlisted the aid and cooperation of all the children within the household. We had weekly family meetings and frequent "conferences," many decisions were made jointly. We arranged the children's sleeping quarters by age rather than by relationship; we made every effort to avoid partiality toward our own children; we petitioned grandparents and friends to treat the children as much alike as possible.

In public we tried to give the impression of being one

family. We never referred to the children as stepchildren and they called us by the parental names, that is, Mom and Dad. People sometimes asked which child belonged to which parent; these inquiries were sidestepped when possible. Except when strictly necessary (for example, when medical histories were needed), my husband and I tried to behave as if all the children were the offspring of our relationship.

The question of last name became an issue. My children asked quite early in the marriage to have their names changed to that of their "new" father because it embarrassed them to have a name different from the rest of us. My husband and I, however, decided to have them wait one year in order to be sure that this was what they really wanted. At the end of the year, we all had the same surname, although, for legal reasons, my husband never adopted my children, nor did I adopt his.

After a time, we noted with satisfaction that we had indeed become one family. This is not to say that we had no problems. There was rivalry and competition among the four boys. Cliques formed. Some of the children, not necessarily my husband's, were closer to my husband; some, not necessarily my own, were closer to me. The problems developed not because we were originally two families; rather, they were the kinds of problems to be found in almost any family.

About the time we were beginning to feel solidarity, we noticed the reconstituted families of our friends and neighbors. We realized that what we were achieving was somewhat unique. Many were not faring so well. Some of these reconstituted families were sharply divided. Stepsibs had poor or no relationships with each other; stepparents and stepchildren avoided each other or displayed open hostility. Several remarriages were in jeopardy because of obvious disharmony.

In an effort to understand why our family seemed to have gained a sense of oneness while others had not, I began to observe the families and to ask questions. From this initial curiosity and inquiry came this study. The first question was: What was there about our reconstituted family and others which also appeared to be successful that differed from families which were not consolidating? Second: Which ingredients within my family led to strong primary-group ties? I realized that reconstituted families achieve such ties only when they make conscious efforts in that direction. A primary family, on the other hand, does this on an unconscious level.

Not every facet of a topic can be covered in any one study. I have tried in this one to deal with what I consider to be the most important aspects of the reconstituted family. Some of my information came from the people I interviewed; some came from insights I gained beyond the answers to my straightforward questions. Information also came from my own life experience and from informal observations. I have tried to put the information from these sources together in a coherent manner so as to present a picture of how remarried people and their children constitute (or fail to constitute) a family. Contrary to my expectations, I found that most of the members of reconstituted families considered their families to be quite successful. I am aware, of course, that the people I talked with were self-selected and that, therefore, a bias was operative. Those who were not successful were less likely to talk with me. Nevertheless, the stereotype of the unsuccessful reconstituted family was not, in general, upheld.

Certain people helped to make this book possible and I would like to take this opportunity to thank them. Professor Marie Haug was more than patient with my ignorance, and I should like to thank her for the many hours she gave me painstakingly explaining statistical procedures. Professor Irwin Deutscher tried to shake me out of complacency and mediocrity and forced me to look beyond the data and into deeper meanings. At times his insistence was frustrating and I am sure I have not succeeded to the point he would have liked. I especially want to thank Professor Marvin B. Sussman, who was always there to put the pieces together and point out connections I had missed. His clarity and vision directed me toward pathways I never would have found alone. I also wish to thank the people at Nelson-Hall, especially Dorothy Anderson and William Steubing, who were also kind, patient, and insightful. Finally, my thanks to my dear friend and mentor, the late Professor Erwin O. Smigel, who gave me kindness, intuition, and interest, and who was a source of encouragement and support.

1/The special problems of the reconstituted family

Although there are many sociological and psychological studies of marriage, of the family, of children, and of divorce, there are few studies of remarriage and almost none of stepchild-stepparent or stepsibling relationships. This study will examine these relationships.

The earliest studies[1] of reconstituted families were written in the 1920s; none dealt with more than ten subjects, and all were psychology oriented. Early investigations of a sociological nature were made by Hannah Kuhn,[2] followed by Mudroch, Neuman, and Von Lincke in the 1930s.[3] These studies, involving as many as a thousand subjects, were written primarily to illustrate the difficult role of the stepmother.

Additional studies include one by Fortes, who attempted to link delinquency with various kinds of abnormal family patterns, step-families (reconstituted families) included.[4] There have been several studies done by social workers.[5] The more recent ones have stressed psychological factors.[6]

William C. Smith published an important book in the

area of remarriage and step-relations in which he reviewed most of the previous writings on this subject. He also presented several additional hypotheses, none of which had been tested empirically.[7] Jessie Bernard deals with step-family relationships, but from the point of view of people associated with the remarried couples rather than from the position of the family members themselves.[8] William J. Goode contributed to the understanding of these relationships by his discussion of the adjustments required of stepmothers.[9]

Bowerman and Irish, in their study of over two thousand stepchildren, found that there was a greater amount of "stress, ambivalence, and low cohesiveness"[10] in step-families than in primary families. They also found that the role of stepmother was more difficult than that of step-father, and that stepdaughters had a more difficult adjustment to make than stepsons. Anne W. Simon detailed the pressures and problems of life in step-families, but did not seek sociological explanations for the difficulties.[11]

There have been studies and articles on step-relations which emphasized psychological factors, but which lacked empirical data.[12] However, there is no major literature on the sociological factors which affect step-relationships. The object of this study is to fill this void, to explain the dynamics of the reconstituted family, its possible effects on society, and the societal influences upon it.

Most remarriages, especially those which include young children, take place between divorced people,[13] and social scientists have theorized for many years on the effects of divorce and remarriage on children. Most of the speculations, however, have been impressionistic.[14] Recently, sociologists[15] have begun to turn their attention to remarriage, its visibility having been heightened because of its increasing prevalence.

Divorce rates are increasing. In 1960 there were 28 divorced men for every 1,000 men living with their wives; by 1970 this ratio had increased to 35 per 1,000. There were 42 divorced women to every 1,000 women living with their husbands in 1960, compared to a ratio of 60 per 1,000 in 1970.[16] In 1965 marital terminations, exclusive of death, involved 1,588,000 persons, including children. Of every five divorces in the United States today, three are characterized by the presence of children.[17]

The divorce rate, which appears to be rising by approximately 8 percent each year, has resulted in an increase in the number of remarriages. In addition, the proportion of remarriages involving children under the age of eighteen has also risen sharply. Although the statistics are incomplete and difficult to amass and assemble, not to mention to interpret, it is estimated that there are approximately eight million "reconstituted" American families and that there are some seven million children living with a stepparent.[18]

In the past, although remarriage was encouraged between widowed people, American culture rejected remarried couples if one or both of the partners had been divorced. Clergymen were disinclined to perform remarriage ceremonies; laws were passed which were intended to discourage such unions. Today the views toward remarriage are changing in response to life in a highly mobile, urbanized, and industrialized society. Such a society facilitates divorce without providing the satisfactions which marriage provides. Thus, remarriage is rapidly becoming more prevalent.

Almost one of every eight married persons has been married before; one in every five marriages is a remarriage for at least one of the partners. Within five years of divorce, three-quarters of all divorced people are remarried. Among the widowed, one-half of the men and one-quarter of the women are remarried within the same period.[19]

The decided increase in divorce and remarriage and the number of children involved justify the study of these phenomena. Although divorce and remarriage are increasing rapidly, they are often perceived by society as deviant because of society's inability to cope with them. Step-families are difficult for Americans to categorize. No general characteristics are attributed to them, and they are viewed with disapproval and suspicion. Society has devised no formal behaviors for divorce and remarriage, thus divorce is often thought of as failure and remarriage as problematical at best. Society does not appear able to deal with divorce or remarriage in the ritualized manner with which it copes with birth, marriage, and death, which society views as natural stages in the life cycle. There seems to be little realization of the fact that people change and grow all through life, and with such change and growth new needs and goals develop, often requiring different marital partners and life styles. This becomes even more true as the human life span increases. It is not inconceivable that divorce and remarriage will come to be part of what will be considered the "natural" life cycle.

It is important, then, to study reconstituted families, because the increases in divorce and remarriage rates in the United States are threatening to many people and because we have no institutionalized ways of integrating these families into society. This study hopes to provide the reader with a greater understanding of the step-family and the process by which it achieves integration and solidarity. Such understanding may provide a basis for societal acceptance.

One important question that this study seeks to answer is: How do the members of a new family go about forming themselves into a primary group? American sociologist Charles Horton Cooley was the first to use the term *primary group* in such a way as to give it meaning for sociology today.[20] Cooley defined a primary group as a small group of persons characterized by face-to-face association, close and intimate contact, cooperation, and affectional ties. He said that such groups are basic in the formation of the human being's social nature and ideals. Close association led to the fusing of individuals into a common whole, so that the self became an integral part of the common life of the group. Cooley did not believe that such groups are completely harmonious; he felt they are also competitive and differentiated. However, the disharmony is tempered with sympathy, the feeling of allegiance, and common goals.

Among such groups, according to Cooley, are the family, childrens' play groups, and the neighborhood or community. He called them "primary" because they are the first groups in which people experience social unity and because they are relatively permanent; out of the learning acquired in such groups an individual is able later to form relationships in other groups.

For a long while the term *primary group* was in disuse: indeed, it was also in mild disrepute.[21] Recently, however, it has been reinterpreted[22] and reinstated as a useful concept for sociology. Lee believes that the four properties which identify the primary group, as Cooley defined it, are necessary conditions for its existence. The properties are: (1) the group must have shared ideals; (2) the group must be the first such group in an individual's experience; (3) there must be personal and intimate association: and (4) there must be a psychological feeling of "we-ness." (The second condition, however, is not really necessary. If it were, no reconstituted family could ever succeed.)

In sum, then, a primary group is one characterized by frequent, intimate, face-to-face interaction in which qualities of competition and hostility exist, tempered by feelings of love, sympathy, and shared goals. The prototype primary group is the family which, through the process of socialization, is able to form the social nature of individuals so that they are enabled to live within a society in relative harmony. (Sociologists define socialization as a basic social process through which an individual becomes integrated into his social group by learning the goals, values, attitudes, behaviors, and beliefs that his group considers proper. The basic process occurs during childhood, but it continues all through life.) The remarried couple and their children from past and present marriages must develop into a primary group if they are to live peacefully within their society and within their own home.

Classical sociologist Georg Simmel tried to explain how societies form and maintain order.[23] In order to examine our question we might look at the way Simmel described what he called "the process of sociation"—the development of stable patterns of relationships between individuals through social interaction and social communication.

Simmel said that we are able to communicate and interact because we are able to recognize each other as human beings. Recognition comes because we can discern similarities with and differences between each other. The similarities allow us to think of others as like ourselves; the differences allow us to think of others as unique individuals. We cannot ever know another human being perfectly because of our own uniqueness and the uniqueness of others. But, depending on how many similarities are perceived, relationships can become very close. The question is, then: What are the ways and means used by members of step-families to formulate themselves into "real" families—primary groups? Is it true that the more alike the backgrounds of the individual members, the greater the probability that they will be successful?

Most step-families appear to be primary families, but they do not, at least at the beginning, feel like one unit. The problem is a result, largely, of a need for time to assume new roles—in this case, those of mother, father, and siblings. In part, of course, step-family members know something about their new roles because they have been family members before. Nevertheless, they have not been step-family members before and are generally unsure of themselves in their new statuses.

Furthermore, all the actors in the reconstituted family must attempt this transformation simultaneously. This is difficult not only because society does not know how to treat them, but also because they are not quite sure themselves what is required of them and no one in the family group can help or advise them. The primary parent's status as parent in a reconstituted family has been compromised. "Father," after all, is the reciprocal of "mother," and when mother is no longer a member of the family, father's fatherhood is diminished or questioned. He is no longer a warrantable parent and cannot offer the assurances to the woman to whom he is now married, nor to his own or his wife's children, that they are performing their new roles adequately. Thus, the desired transformation into a "family" is complicated by the absence of assurances from one another and from outsiders that they are succeeding. No one knows exactly what "success" as a member of a reconstituted family means.

One major area discussed in this book is how reconstituted families come to see themselves and to be seen by others as primary groups. In primary families, within which parents and children have known each other all of the children's lives, there is a unity which evolves slowly, without deliberation. This, however, is manifestly impossible in families of remarriage, where the members have separate histories and memories, and different concepts of roles, values, norms, and goals. Solidarity, the concept members of a family have of themselves as one functioning unit, must be carefully cultivated if it is to be achieved. Status, duties, and privileges must be redefined in the context of the new family. "The achievement of a successful relationship between acquired parents and children has traditionally been considered one of the most difficult of all human assignments."[24]

The second major area the book deals with is the "problems" area. This includes problems that relate to the entire family as one unit, to each of the dyads involved (that is, to husband and wife, stepparent and stepchild, and stepsibs), and to the people outside of the family who populate its world.[7]

What are the specific problems which arise in the step-family? How do they differ from problems in the primary family? What are the factors in society that cause or exacerbate these problems?[25] In what ways (if at all) do the norms of the society in which the reconstituted family is embedded facilitate the solution to these problems?

Reconstituted families share many of the "normal" problems of primary families; yet they also contain unique problem areas which have been defined by Jessie Bernard.[26] Among the most prominent are: the self-consciousness of adults and children; the embarrassment of maintaining a relationship with the living biological parent who is of the same sex as the stepparent; the question of adoption; rivalry between stepparent and stepchild; competition between stepbrothers and stepsisters and between parents and stepparents; and money as a source of resentment.

While these are primarily psychological problems, they have a societal genesis, which should be explored and understood. This point of view is succinctly expressed by Ruth S. Cavan:

> Society has condemned and ignored [remarriage and divorce]; it has not sympathized and helped. There is no uniform collective attitude toward divorce or the divorced person. Some of the emotional disturbance attending a divorce is generated by this undefined situation and the conflict between the traditional opinion that marriage is inviolate and the actual fact that many people are breaking their marriages.[27]

In this study, the following assumptions have been made about reconstituted families:

1. The reconstituted family has unusual and difficult interpersonal and intrapersonal problems, not the least of which is its categorization by society and by itself as deviant.

2. Reconstituted families must make conscious efforts to establish themselves as entities.

3. The relationship between the stepchild and the stepparent is generally unsatisfactory to the individuals involved and to society in general.

4. Reconstituted families exhibit greater stress, ambivalence, and lack of cohesiveness than primary families.

5. The stepmother and the stepdaughter have a more difficult adjustment than the stepfather and the stepson.

6. The lack of institutionalization and the disapproval of divorce, of remarriage, and of reconstituted families in the United States, despite the prevalence of these three phenomena, are detrimental to the achievement of good steprelationships. These negative attitudes exist not only within the society toward the remarried couple and toward their children, but also within the family unit itself. There is a strong probability that in the absence of the approval of significant others (those people who strongly influence an individual), the formation of a group into a family is decidedly inhibited.

7. The most detrimental factors in the reciprocal role relationship of the stepparent and the stepchild are hostility, competition, and jealousy, all of which arise from feelings of insecurity and role confusion on the part of each, and originating in, and exacerbated by, the society. The presence of these factors may well be symptomatic of a structural problem—the shortened time span for moving through the role sequences as the steprelatives attempt to form themselves into a family.

2/Description of the sample

Because of the personal nature of the problem, the paucity of previous research, and the difficulty in conceptualization, it was decided that this study should be primarily descriptive. Therefore, the sample size was limited to a small number of reconstituted families with whom a more in-depth study could be conducted.

The names of the eighty-eight families of the sample were drawn from the Marriage License Bureau of Cuyahoga County in Cleveland, Ohio. Cleveland was chosen because it is a "middle" American city, both geographically and emotionally. Only Caucasian couples were selected who had remarried during the years 1965-1968, who were under forty-five years of age, and who had children under eighteen at the time of the remarriage. Couples married during this period were chosen because a sufficient time would have elapsed for the marriage to have established some pattern of interaction; at the same time, the remarriage would be recent enough for the subjects to be able to recall clearly the events that had transpired during the marriage.

Table 2.1 shows the composition of the families. As expected, because of the American custom of awarding custody of the children to the mother, the mother-based family is overrepresented. When the households contain the man's children, it is almost always because the man had been widowed.

TABLE 2.1

Composition of Households		
Composition	Percent of Households	
	percent	number
Husband and wife only*	20	(18)
Husband, wife, her children only	38	(33)
Husband, wife, his children only	15	(13)
Husband, wife, and both sets of children	27	(24)
Total	100	(88)

*This situation existed when the wife had no children from a previous marriage and the man's children lived with his previous wife.

The interviews were in two parts. First, the couple was interviewed together to obtain demographic information (age, religion, occupation, income, etc.). Then, one or the other was asked to leave the room and complete a written questionnaire. During the time that one partner was filling out the questionnaire, the interviewer asked open-ended questions of the other partner, who remained in the room. The answers were tape recorded. When the oral interview was completed, the second spouse retired to fill out the same written questionnaire while the first answered the same open-ended questions.

My interest centered primarily on the reconstituted family as a unit. I wanted to know whether the members had an image of themselves as an entity and the process through which they had or had not attained this solidarity. Integration, then, was the primary focus of interest. Integration is defined as the linkages and relationships within the reconstituted family as a whole. My concern was with the nature and extent of the linkages and bonds between family members. Seven component elements reflect different ways in which family members are bound together and to the group as a whole. The seven theoretical components are:

1. *Joint family participation:* the extent of interaction of family members as they participate in common activities.

2. *Communication and joint decision-making:* the degree to which family members communicate, discuss, and jointly participate in decisions about matters concerning the family.

3. *Affectional integration:* the degree of positive affect members express toward one another. Concern here is with sentiments of empathy, closeness, identification, and satisfaction expressed within the family context.

4. *Goal integration:* the degree to which family members subordinate their interests to those of the family as a whole.

5. *Normative integration:* the extent of the family's control or influence over individuals in the family.

6. *Consensual integration:* the extent of agreement among family members regarding matters relevant to the family.

7. *Parental interest:* the extent of overt parental concern for, or interest in, the offspring of the family.

In addition to my interest in the family's integration as a unit, I was also interested in certain other relationships both *per se* and as they affected the family as an entity. Therefore I examined the relationship between the husband and wife, the relationships among stepsiblings, and the relationships between stepparents and stepchildren. It was also possible that outsiders influenced the family unit, and so the attitudes of family and close friends, and the attitudes of former spouses were examined. Finally, because I felt that certain other variables would affect the integration of the family, I compared the subjects in terms of social class, religion, occupation, and education.

Tables 2.2, 2.3, 2.4, and 2.5 reveal that the mean age for remarried men was 35 and the mean age for women was 34.6. Sixty-two percent of the men and 39 percent of the women had had some college education. Forty-nine percent of the men and 53 percent of the women were Protestant, while 32 percent and 31 percent, respectively, were Roman Catholic. Less than 10 percent of both men and women were Jewish or unaffiliated. Fifty-nine percent of the remarried women were housewives. The remaining 41 percent were fairly evenly distributed among the blue collar, white collar, and professional-managerial classes. Husbands were similarly

11

distributed among the three classes. The families had a mean income of $17,735, with 12 percent under $10,000 and 12 percent over $30,000. Approximately 60 percent of both men and women had been divorced, 24 percent of the men and 19 percent of the women had been widowed, and 15 percent and 22 percent, respectively, had never been married before. Of those who had been married, 43 percent of the men had been married more than fifteen years and 43 percent of the women had been married between five and ten years. Approximately 40 percent of both men and women had children between the ages of five and thirteen, there being equal numbers of girls and boys.

TABLE 2.2

Demographic Description of the Sample				
Characteristic	Husbands		Wives	
	percent	number	percent	number
Age				
20-29	8	(7)	19	(17)
30-39	30	(26)	45	(40)
40 and over	62	(55)	35	(31)
Total ascertained	100	(88)	99**	(88)
Mean age	35.0		34.6	
Education				
Less than high school	5	(4)	11	(10)
Completed high school	33	(29)	49	(44)
Some college	25	(22)	19	(16)
Completed college	22	(19)	11	(10)
Some graduate school	6	(5)	3	(3)
Completed graduate school	9	(8)	6	(5)
Total	100	(87)*	99	(88)
Religion				
Protestant	49	(43)	53	(46)
Catholic	32	(28)	31	(27)
Jewish	9	(8)	8	(7)
Unaffiliated	9	(8)	8	(7)
Total	99	(87)*	100	(87)*
Occupation				
Housewife			59	(52)
Blue collar	36	(32)	10	(9)
White collar	36	(32)	18	(16)
Professional/Manager	27	(24)	13	(11)
Total	99	(88)	100	(88)

*One answer not ascertained.
**Total percent less than 100 due to rounding.

TABLE 2.3

	Families	
Income	percent	number
$ 5,000—$ 9,999	12	(11)
$10,000—$14,999	31	(27)
$15,000—$19,999	31	(27)
$20,000—$29,999	14	(12)
Over $30,000	12	(11)
Total	100	(88)
Mean income	$17,735	

TABLE 2.4

Marital History

Previous marital status	Husbands		Wives	
	percent	number	percent	number
Divorced	61	(54)	59	(51)
Widowed	24	(21)	19	(17)
Never married before	15	(13)	22	(20)
Total	100	(88)	100	(88)
Length of previous marriage				
Less than 5 years	12	(11)	17	(15)
5 to 10 years	26	(22)	31	(27)
11 to 15 years	16	(14)	15	(13)
Over 15 years	31	(28)	15	(13)
Never married before	15	(13)	22	(20)
Total	100	(88)	100	(88)

TABLE 2.5

Children from Previous Marriages

Ages of Children	Husbands		Wives	
	percent	number	percent	number
Boys				
Less than 5 years	16	(8)	11	(5)
5 to 13 years	38	(19)	45	(21)
14 to 18 years	20	(10)	13	(6)
Mixed age group	16	(8)	23	(11)
Over 18	10	(5)	8	(4)
Total parents	100	(50)	100	(47)
Girls				
Less than 5 years	13	(7)	17	(9)
5 to 13 years	33	(17)	38	(20)
14 to 18 years	23	(12)	9	(5)
Mixed age group	21	(11)	28	(15)
Over 18	10	(5)	8	(4)
Total parents	100	(52)	100	(53)

Of the eighty-eight husbands in the sample, sixteen had no children from a previous marriage. Of the seventy-two fathers, 54 percent had their children living with them in the household of the second marriage. Of the eighty-eight wives in the sample, twenty-two had no children from a previous marriage. Of the sixty-six mothers, 89 percent had their children living with them in the household of the second marriage.

Comparative figures for income and occupation were unavailable, but in several respects the sample is not unlike the general population in Cleveland. For example, Protestants and those with no religious affiliation make up 55 percent of the population of Cuyahoga County, of which Greater Cleveland is a part. Catholics represent 37 percent of the population, and 8 percent of the population is Jewish.[1] The sample in the study comprises 51 percent Protestant, 31 percent Catholic, 9 percent Jewish, and 9 percent unaffiliated.

In Greater Cleveland, 39 percent of the population finished high school, 16 percent attended college, and 17 percent completed college.[2] In this sample, 41 percent completed high school, 21 percent attended college, and 22 percent graduated from college.

The median age for remarrying men across the nation is 38.3 years and 34.0 years for women.[3] The mean age for this sample was 35.0 for men and 34.6 for women.

The research families, then, are reasonably representative of families in an urban setting in the United States. It is possible, therefore, that the data presented herein may be valid for other reconstituted families. However, statistics for the remarried population of the United States are not obtainable, therefore no claim is made that this study is a systematic one, the results of which would apply to all remarried couples with children from previous marriages.

SOCIAL CLASS STRUCTURE OF THE SAMPLE

Every complex society is also a stratified society, and social class position everywhere is a potential influence in determining social behavior, values, attitudes, and goals. Social class position becomes even more important as other differentiating statuses, such as religious, ethnic, regional, and racial, decline. Thus, as Americans become more alike in these statuses, as the farmer comes to act like the city dweller, as the black man becomes more like the white man, as the Polish-American becomes like the Scottish-American, social class becomes the key discriminating characteristic.[4]

Social class, then, was considered of major significance, so the sample was divided into classes and the characteristics of each class were noted.

In order to place each family in one of three social classes, working, middle, and upper middle, each husband and wife was asked to record how far he or she had gone in school and how much annual income the family had. Occupations were categorized separately for men and women into blue collar (truck driver, electrician, plumber, etc.), white collar (salesperson, office worker, small businessman, etc.), and professional-managerial (doctor, teacher, lawyer, corporate executive, etc.). According to the category the subject placed himself or herself in (education, income, or occupation), the subject received a score.

For example, if a man had had some college and his wife had had some high school, the education scores would be 5 for the husband and 3 for the wife. If their combined income was $21,000, their income score would be 5. If the husband were employed as credit manager of a bank and the wife worked as a bookkeeper, he would score 4 and she would score 3 on the occupation scale. If we then combine their scores and divide by 5, the resulting score would place them in the middle class.

Table 2.6 shows how the sample was divided into three social classes. Nineteen percent were in the working class, 55 percent were in the middle class, and 26 percent were in the upper middle class.

TABLE 2.6

Socioeconomic Class		
Class	Families	
	percent	number
Working	19	(17)
Middle	55	(48)
Upper middle	26	(23)

I then attempted to determine the characteristics of these classes in terms of age, religion, length of previous marriage, previous marital status, residence of children, and major problems.

AGE

Table 2.7 shows that 70 percent of the working class people, 55 percent of the middle class, and 28 percent of the upper middle class were under forty. These figures imply that the lower the class, the greater the likelihood of remarriage at a younger age.

TABLE 2.7

Social Class and Age						
	Age					
Social Class*	40 and under		Over 40		Total	
	percent	number	percent	number	percent	number
Working	70	(24)	30	(10)	100	(34)
Middle	55	(53)	45	(43)	100	(96)
Upper middle	28	(13)	72	(33)	100	(46)
Total		(90)		(86)		(176)

*The categories of husband and wife were collapsed for most of the variables in this section in order to increase the number of cases in each cell. This was based on the assumption that the separation by sex was not necessary since husbands and wives are generally in the same social class. The tables were drawn in the two possible ways and almost no difference could be found. Therefore, in this section the sex categories have been eliminated in most tables.

RELIGION

I compared social class with the expectation that there would be more Protestants in the upper middle class than in either of the other two classes, and more Catholics in the working class than in either of the other two classes.

TABLE 2.8

Social Class and Religion										
	Religion									
Social class	Protestant		Catholic		Jewish		Unaffiliated		Total	
	%	#	%	#	%	#	%	#	%	#
Working	50	(17)	35	(12)	3	(1)	12	(4)	100	(34)
Middle	48	(45)	36	(34)	10	(9)	6	(6)	100	(94)
Upper middle	60	(27)	20	(9)	10	(5)	10	(5)	100	(46)
Total		89		55		15		15		175*

*One couple did not state their religious preference.

Table 2.8 shows that the expectation was not realized. There was little religious difference between the three classes of remarried parents although there was a slight tendency for more of the upper middle class to be Protestant and fewer to be Catholic.

LENGTH OF THE PREVIOUS MARRIAGE

TABLE 2.9

Social Class and Length of Previous Marriage

Social class	Length of previous marriage					
	Ten years or less		Over 10 years		Total	
	percent	number	percent	number	percent	number
Working	72	(18)	28	(7)	100	(25)
Middle	48	(38)	52	(42)	100	(80)
Upper middle	40	(19)	50	(19)	100	(38)
Total		75		68		143*

*Thirteen of the men and 20 of the women had never been married before.

Table 2.9 indicates almost no difference between the middle class and the upper middle class in terms of the length of previous marriages. However, of the working class people, 72 percent had been previously married ten years or less and only 28 percent had been married over ten years. This supports the evidence in Table 2.7, showing that the working-class people divorced and remarried earlier than the middle- or upper-middle-class people. It was also true that working-class young people married younger than their counterparts in the other classes.

PREVIOUS MARITAL STATUS

It was anticipated that the greatest percentage of divorced people would be of the working class, because studies have shown that divorce rates are lowest among professionals, moderate for the middle classes, and highest for the semiskilled.[5] It was further anticipated that the percentage of widowed people would vary inversely with class; that is, the higher the social class, the less likelihood of widowhood because the probability is that the highest social class receives better medical care and is in less hazardous occupations. Finally, it was anticipated that the highest percentage of those who had never been married before would be in the upper middle class and the lowest in the working class.

TABLE 2.10

	Social Class and Previous Marital Status							
	Previous marital status							
Social class	Divorced		Widowed		Single		Total	
	%	#	%	#	%	#	%	#
Working	53	(18)	26	(9)	21	(7)	100	(34)
Middle	61	(58)	19	(18)	20	(20)	100	(96)
Upper middle	63	(29)	23	(11)	14	(6)	100	(46)
Total		(105)		(38)		(33)		(176)

The findings on Table 2.10 do not bear out the expectations. There was no difference among the social classes in any of the three categories.

RESIDENCE OF CHILDREN FROM PREVIOUS MARRIAGES

For this variable, husbands and wives were examined separately. Because of the norms of the society, women are more likely to obtain custody of their children after divorce. I anticipated that men would, in all classes, be less likely to have their children living with them. I expected, however, that for women, the higher the social class, the greater would be the probability of the children living in the same home with the mother, but that this difference between the classes would be small.

TABLE 2.11

	Social Class and Childrens' Residences					
	Children's Residence					
Social class	Living at home		Not living at home		Total	
	percent	number	percent	number	percent	number
Husbands						
Working	38	(5)	62	(8)	100	(13)
Middle	63	(26)	37	(15)	100	(41)
Upper middle	45	(8)	55	(10)	100	(18)
Total		(39)		(33)		(72*)
Wives						
Working	77	(10)	23	(3)	100	(13)
Middle	88	(30)	12	(4)	100	(34)
Upper middle	100	(19)	0	(0)	100	(19)
Total		(59)		(7)		(66*)

*Sixteen of the men and 22 of the women did not have children from previous marriages.

Table 2.11 reveals that the middle-class men and upper-middle-class women were more likely to have their children living in their homes than people in other categories. These were the expected findings. The higher the social class, the greater the probability that the children would be living with their mothers. Women are more likely to have their children living with them than men. Indeed, given the fact that only 24 percent of the men in the sample were widowed, it was surprising that the percent of men who had their children living with them was as high as the table indicates.

PERCEPTION OF MAJOR PROBLEMS

In the eighty-eight families in the sample there were no differences by social classes or by sex in the perception of the major family problems. With one exception all groups felt that child-rearing was the primary problem and outsiders' influences was the second major problem. The exception was the middle-class husbands group, who selected money as the second most bothersome problem.

It appears, then, that for remarried people the greatest difficulties were encountered with child-rearing and outsiders' influence, irrespective of class or sex. This finding contradicts that of Blood and Wolfe.[6] These authors found that for first time married housewives, money was the source of the greatest disagreement, with children ranking second. Their category which is most comparable to "outsiders' influence" is "in-laws," which ranks fifth in the list of areas of disagreement in this study.

The remarried people in this sample, in their efforts to form a reconstituted family, were inclined to put aside the more common problems of money in order to concentrate on their own and each other's children. Furthermore, it is likely that the stress from outsiders may have been due to self-consciousness about divorce and remarriage; remarried people were aware of other people's opinions of them.

3/Family integration and demographic factors

Because a basic concern of this study is the transformation of the reconstituted families into primary groups, the major dependent variable is the integration of the reconstituted family. Family integration is a total pattern, and the relationship between any two members of the family influences, and is influenced by, the "unity of interacting personalities."[1] Much of what occurs within primary families on a subconscious level which makes for primary group feelings probably occurs on a conscious level within reconstituted families. The divorced adults and even the children of divorced parents had some experience with marital failure prior to the second marriage, and most expressed a strong desire to succeed in this second attempt. Even if the first marriage ended because of a death, most of the people in this sample were aware of areas in which that marriage could have been better. Some of them expressed this quite directly:

There were certain things in my first marriage that weren't really correct and I think Helen and I get along on these things. I had some problems in my first marriage and I'm always quite aware of them.

You have to be sure of yourself before you re-marry, sure of what you want. You ought to know what to look for so you don't repeat old mistakes.

Our marriage is excellent. We found out in our first marriages where we made mistakes.

I'm a lot happier than [I was] in my first marriage. It's better because we learned from our first marriages. In my first marriage, [I involved myself in] arguments, well, like my whole life depended on it. I had to defend myself. It got very vicious. I think I learned not to take things as seriously.

Others were very practical about their second marriages, while keeping in mind the problems of the first one.

I would consider this marriage content, maybe. I wouldn't say we're extremely happy. We have our times. If this were my first marriage, I don't think I'd stand for it. When you mature a little bit more, you accept a little bit more. If we were both younger, I don't know if we would put up with [each other].

If I had a friend who was getting married again I'd tell him to be sure the girl he was marrying would be a good mother, would be able to cope with the kids. That's more important than romantic love the second time around. Maybe that sounds awful, but it's true.

Two husbands expressed the fear they had of a second marriage because of the failure of the first one.

I was a little afraid when we first got married. I worried it would be like the first marriage. But I'm a little bit older than [I was in] the first marriage.

We were quite doubtful because of what had happened with first marriages.

Three other husbands spoke of the self-conscious efforts they felt had to be made in forming a reconstituted family.

I think we are aware of it [the need to act and to be seen as one family]. Sometimes I think we try harder not to make it obvious that we are trying because we don't want to put an edge on it. Now it seems to be developing that we don't have to [try so hard]; we can relax a little more that attitude of proving that we care.

You have to be able to give a lot more than in a normal marriage. There's a lot more problems. You have to make special efforts to do right.

It's much harder work than you think. You have to always be on your toes, alert to what the kids are really saying. This I don't think is really any different than [in] normal families. It's just that the problems that the kids in a second marriage bring up are less obvious. You become more aware that these kids have emotional problems.

The above are only a few of the remarks many of the subjects made in regard to their awareness of past errors and their conscious efforts to make their second marriages more successful than the first ones. It was assumed, therefore, that the subjects would be able to describe what they were doing (and how they were doing it) to achieve a feeling of being a family.

FAMILY INTEGRATION SCORE

A Family Integration Score (FIS), given to each family, was calculated in the following way. Each husband and wife was asked to rate the closeness of the total family on a continuum from "Very close" to "Very distant." During the oral part of the interview, each couple was asked to discuss their feelings about the family as a group. In addition, I rated the integration of the family, basing my score on the oral discussion and on observation. Thus, five subscores were obtained and were combined into a Family Integration Score, which was categorized as "Low," "Moderate," and "High."

TABLE 3.1

Couples' Ratings on a Continuum of Family Integration				
Rating	Husbands		Wives	
	percent	number	percent	number
Low	18	(16)	16	(14)
Moderate	30	(27)	36	(32)
High	52	(45)	48	(42)

Table 3.1 shows that there was no meaningful difference between husbands' and wives' self-ratings. Table 3.2 below, however, shows that the investigator's evaluations differed from the self-ratings, with the likelihood that the investigator gave lower ratings than the subjects gave themselves.

TABLE 3.2

Investigator's Ratings of Family Integration		
Rating	Percent of Families	
	percent	number
Low	22	(20)
Moderate	35	(31)
High	43	(37)

TABLE 3.3

Combined Family Integration Scores (FIS)		
Rating	Percent of Families	
	percent	number
Low	21	(19)
Moderate	34	(30)
High	45	(39)

Table 3.3 reveals the FIS after the five subscores had been combined. Twenty-one percent of the families were rated "Low"; 34 percent were rated "Moderate"; and 45 percent were rated "High."

FAMILY INTEGRATION AS A DEPENDENT VARIABLE

There are many variables which theoretically could have an effect on family integration. It was, of course, not feasible to examine all of them or even to know what all of them might be. Several were selected as being of probable importance, and they will be discussed in this chapter. The independent variables are: the husband's and the wife's ages at the time of the remarriage; the husband's and the wife's religions; a difference of religion between the marital pair; the educational levels of the husband and the wife; the previous marital status of the husband and wife; the length of the previous marriages; the presence or absence of children from the present marriage; and social class.

Some of the independent variables could affect the dependent variable, family integration, differentially by sex; for others, the sex of the subject was unimportant. If there was no difference between the husbands and the wives, the sex of the respondent was ignored in this report.

Age

It was expected that the ages[2] of the husbands and wives at the time of the remarriage would vary inversely with the degree of family integration, that is, the younger the couple, the greater the probability of a high FIS. This was anticipated because, in general, remarriage, especially when children under eighteen years of age are involved, requires a great deal of flexibility on the part of the adults. In addition, younger people are usually considered more capable and more willing to make adjustments in their attitudes and behaviors. Therefore, I anticipated that younger remarrieds would be able to achieve greater family integration than older people. The findings revealed that 53 percent of the parents who were under forty were in the "High" FIS category compared to 36 percent of those who were over forty. There is, then, a moderate inverse relationship between the age of the stepparent and the amount of integration achieved in the reconstituted families studied. (See Appendix B for a discussion of the statistical procedures used.)

Religion

There was no reason to expect higher degrees of integration in any one of the religious categories. Although Catholic marriages are more likely to stay intact because of religious prohibition against divorce, this intactness would not qualify as a measure of family integration. In point of fact, one very unhappy couple, by their own definition, was Catholic. In addition, most of the Catholics in the sample had been divorced; therefore, presumably they did not subscribe to their church's edict against divorce.

Religion might be expected to have an effect on integration if the remarrying partners were of different faiths. This effect on family integration might be a by-product of outsiders' disapproval; or it might be a factor in and of itself, especially if one or both of the partners held strong religious convictions. However, it was not expected to be meaningful. As anticipated, it was found that neither the religion of the family nor a difference of religion of members of the family was a factor in family integration.

In general, it seems that among the subjects, religion was rarely a point of issue. Even in interreligious marriages many husbands and wives noted that religion was not an important factor in their relationship. Some comments were:

"We disagree on religion. We don't fight about it, we each know how the other feels."

"She practices her religion and I practice mine."

"There's no particular problem about religion although Penny's a Catholic and I'm not."

"My daughter is being raised as a Catholic, and his three as Jewish. There's no problem about that. My husband has even taken her to catechism class and she's gone with him to temple."

"There was some strain because of the different religious backgrounds, but it just took getting used to."

In five of the eighty-eight marriages studied, either the husband or the wife converted to the partner's religion. Some of their remarks were as follows:

"My kids and I converted to Judaism and I think that helped a lot. It makes a lot of difference. Someone has to

convert. It was good for the children to eliminate some confusion. I'm glad I did it."

"At first we disagreed about religion. We worked it out
by going to my church. She's very accommodating about it.
The church is important to me. We both like the minister and
the kids are happy there."

"I'm very proud that Joe gave up Catholicism for me and
now he's active in our church."

"We used to disagree about religion because I was a
Catholic; but I changed religions and I'm very happy. I'm
very active in his religion, much more so than I ever was as a
Catholic."

In two families, religion per se was not really important,
but the couples used it in a detrimental fashion. In one of
these families, the wife used religion to avoid her husband's
parents, thereby antagonizing her husband. She said:

> I don't like them because of their religion. They
> didn't completely accept his divorce and his mar-
> riage to me.

In the other family, the wife felt that she was being
treated as an outsider by her husband and his children when
the children came to visit on Sundays. This woman became
very active in church activities on Sundays and thus found a
good way to avoid being snubbed. Her husband remarked:

> We disagree about religion. We have problems on
> Sunday. I'm with the kids and she wants to go to
> church all the time. She won't go with us on Sun-
> days. I think it's because she really doesn't want to
> see them, because if I change the visitation day to
> Saturday, she gives me excuses that that's my day
> to clean house. We just don't get to do things as a
> whole family because my wife won't participate.

In terms of religion, the problems seem to center on
depth of religious feelings and/or on participation in the
church, rather than on difference in religion. Even when this
was a family problem, it was not very serious and it did not
occur in many cases. One wife noted:

> Religion is perhaps one area in which we dis-

agree. I am much more religious than my husband. It hasn't led to any real conflicts.

Another husband's remarks indicate how religious difference can be a cohesive factor in a marriage. Recalling his first marriage, he said:

My first wife was very strict on religion. She kept hoping I would come around to her way. It has to be a volunteer thing. My present wife would like me to be Jewish, but she respects me and knows I must make up my own mind.

Although the data revealed that the Protestant and the Catholic families did achieve marginally higher degrees of integration than Jewish and nonaffiliated families, in general, religion did not seem to be an important factor in the integration of the reconstituted family. One wife had been a cloistered nun for eighteen years before her marriage and one husband had been a missionary. Neither partner in these marriages even mentioned religion beyond giving this information in an offhand way.

Previous marital status

On first consideration it was expected that widows and widowers would rate their family integration higher than those who had been divorced or had never been married before, because the involuntary termination of their previous marriages would have predisposed them to making a greater effort to regain former happiness. It was felt that divorced people, having failed in the past, would be more cynical and less optimistic about their second families.

However, a reconsideration of William J. Goode's findings[3] cast doubt on this supposition. Goode found that his remarried divorcees were committed to marriage as a way of life. Furthermore, most of his divorced mothers felt that the mistakes made in the first marriage could be avoided in the second. Goode's subjects believed they had learned from past mistakes, just as the subjects in this study felt they could retain awareness of past problems in order to avoid them.

There was another reason for reconsidering the presumption that the widowed would have higher degrees of integration in second marriages than the divorced. The

27

second marriage of a divorced person has a great advantage over the second marriage of a widowed person because the second marriage will be compared to a marriage that had failed, one in which the partner was unhappy. This is not generally true for those whose first marriages terminated with the death of a partner. Therefore, I preferred to withhold expectations in the matter of the effects of previous marital termination on family integration in reconstituted families, although there was some inclination to suppose that divorced people would attain higher scores.

Data indicate that of those remarried whose previous marriage had terminated in divorce, 34 percent had a "High" FIS compared to 67 percent of those who had been widowed and 50 percent of those who had never been married before. Thus, marital partners who had been previously widowed were more likely to feel they had achieved high integration, while those who had been divorced had the lowest integration scores.

These findings seem to indicate that the initial expectations were more correct than those made upon reconsideration. It seems that family integration was higher in reconstituted families when the marital partners had been widowed rather than divorced or had not been previously married.

The following statements made by some of the people who participated in the study bolster this view. One father who had been widowed mentioned the difficulties involved in bringing up his son alone after the boy's mother died. During the period of his widowhood, his relationship with the boy seriously deteriorated. His son, he said, was instrumental in bringing about his remarriage:

> My boy kept suggesting I marry Joan. It took a long time to get the courage to marry again. Actually my marriage improved my relationship with my son. Without my wife, I'd have been lost with my son.

The previously divorced wife of a widower, commenting on how the experience of her husband's being widowed had helped her second marriage, said:

Ben was a widower and got a good and miserable taste of a housewife's responsibilities, and I knew what it was to be a wage-earner. So we understood each other's responsibilities and problems.

Another previously divorced wife of a widower notes that one happy marriage can lead to another:

We're very, very happy. One reason is that Lenny was happily married before and enjoys married life. He was a wonderful husband to his first wife.

Many subjects who were married to divorced spouses or who were divorced themselves mentioned the problems that derive from ex-mates:

We have our problems, mostly from his ex-wife, with the alimony and support. If anything were to break up the marriage now it would be the money problem because of all the payments to her. I don't mind the support for the children, but I do mind that the money he sends for the kids goes on her back.

A formerly divorced father commented on the difficult relationships between his own children and his stepchildren, which he felt were caused by his ex-wife:

The relationship between her children and my children is bad because of the hostility from my children, especially my daughter. It comes out in many different ways. My daughter resents the fact that my stepdaughters live with me and that she lives in a smaller house and that her mother is difficult, to say the least . . . . The single largest problem we have is my children's hostility to Berry, her children, and the baby—all [encouraged by] my ex-wife.

This man's wife discussed her marriage and her relationship with her stepchildren:

> If the real mother is alive, there's a tremendous
> amount of tension.

The following remarks were made by a man who had not
been married before and who was presently married to a
woman with a young son:

> I consider my relationship with my stepson quite
> often. I work with him in the Indian Guides. This is
> teaching me a lot about parenthood and it is
> something of a shock. It's a little hard to grasp
> when you suddenly find yourself the father of a
> five-year-old boy. You haven't learned from the
> beginning. I'm trying. My stepson is proud of his
> dad. He's very anxious now to do things with me
> and to be like me. I'm still unsure of myself in this
> role, and I'm sometimes a little harsh. Our rela-
> tionship has changed. Taking on a family and a
> young boy was a shock and I think I'm adjusting to
> it. At first I was annoyed and frustrated by him. It
> took getting used to, but I'm used to it now and I
> feel better about it. He and I have gotten closer;
> we have gotten to know each other in many ways.

Length of previous marriage
It was expected that those who had been married long-
est in the first marriage would have settled into routine habits
which would make integration in a new family more difficult. Therefore, it was anticipated that the longer the previous marriage, the lower the degree of integration in the
second marriage.

The findings partially supported the expectation that
family integration would be more readily achieved in those
families where the husbands and wives had been married for
a shorter period of time during the first marriage. However,
the data do not show a clear trend in any direction and are
different for husbands and for wives. Of those husbands previously married less than ten years, 40 percent were in the
"High" FIS category compared to 43 percent of those who
had been married over ten years. On the other hand, of
those wives who had been married less than ten years, 55
percent were in the "High" category compared to 27 per-

cent of those married for a longer period of time.

The wives, apparently, felt integration was highest when they were previously married ten years or less, while there was no difference for husbands in length of previous marriage. The difference for husbands and wives may possibly reflect the presence of young children. Wives who were formerly married less than ten years were more likely to have small children than women who were previously married for a longer time. Such women may have had a greater need to see their second marriages as well-integrated. In contrast, the men who were married a shorter time probably did not have small children living with them. The effects of children's ages will be examined more fully in a later chapter.

Education

Because the sample was small, it had to be dichotomized into those people who had never been to college at all and those who had some college or graduate school education, whether or not completed. It was presumed that integration would be greater when the educational level was higher. Contrary to expectations, education had almost no effect on family integration in the reconstituted families of the sample. Of those parents who had never been to college, 42 percent rated FIS "High" compared to 47 percent of those who had attended college.

This is contradictory to the findings of most studies on the relationship between education and marital success[4]: the more education, the lower the probability of divorce and the higher the probability of good marital adjustment. However, these findings relate to marital happiness, not family integration. Second, they refer to primary marriages, not to reconstituted families. Therefore, any comparison between these studies and the present one may be spurious.

Children from the present marriage

Integration was expected to be higher in families which included children from the present marriage. There is no way of knowing, of course, whether high integration "caused" the couple to have a child together or whether having a child led to increased integration. However, this expectation was predicated on the assumption that remarrying couples are wary and cautious, so that before having a child they would be likely to want some feeling of certainty that their second marriage would be stable. Therefore, the new child or children could be considered an indication of felt stability and integration, rather than a cause of them.

It was found that of those couples who did not have children from the present marriage, 37 percent rated their family integration "High" compared with 54 percent who did have a new family. The findings support the expectation that high family integration is likely to be found in those reconstituted families that contain a child from the new marriage.

Social class

It was expected that family integration would be greater in the higher-social-class families. Given previous findings,[5] it was anticipated that the upper middle class would have the highest family integration, the middle class would follow, and the working class would have the lowest index of FIS.

TABLE 3.4

Social Class and Family Integration								
Social class	FIS							
	Low		Moderate		High		Total	
	%	#	%	#	%	#	%	#
Working class	30	(5)	18	(3)	52	(9)	100	(17)
Middle class	25	(12)	36	(17)	39	(19)	100	(48)
Upper middle class	9	(2)	43	(10)	48	(11)	100	(23)

The findings are not commensurate with the expectations. The working class was found to have the highest integration, the upper middle class followed, and integration was lowest in the middle class. However, it can also be seen that the working-class families tended to have either low or high integration, with few in the "Moderate" category. Middle-class families were rather evenly distributed among the three categories, and the upper-middle-class families appeared to achieve either moderate or high integration, with a very small percentage in the low category.

Because the findings were somewhat unclear, it was decided to see if family integration was affected by a difference between the parents in educational and occupational levels. Income could not be used as a variable because it had not been ascertained separately for husbands and wives.

TABLE 3.5

	FIS							
Educational level	Low		Moderate		High		Total	
	%	#	%	#	%	#	%	#
Difference	18	(10)	32	(18)	80	(27)	100	(55)
No difference	27	(9)	36	(12)	36	(12)	100	(33)

Educational Difference and Family Integration

Note: G=.23

Table 3.5 shows that when there was a difference in educational levels between the husband and the wife in the reconstituted families, 80 percent of these families were in the "High" FIS category compared to 36 percent of the families in which there was no difference in educational level. Past studies on the relationship between educational level and marital success had mixed results. Blood and Wolfe found that wives were happiest when educational levels were equal.[6] Other studies[7] found little relationship between the two variables.

TABLE 3.6

	FIS							
Occupational level	Low		Moderate		High		Total	
	%	#	%	#	%	#	%	#
Difference	45	(6)	39	(5)	15	(2)	100	(13)
No difference	26	(6)	44	(10)	30	(7)	100	(23)
Housewife	13	(7)	29	(15)	58	(30)	100	(52)

Occupational Level and Family Integration

Note: G=.51

When a wife was employed, family integration was higher when the prestige levels of the husband and wife were equal, as shown in Table 3.6. However, if a wife was not employed at all, family integration was highest. Apparently the traditional concept[8] that men should have more education than women, when operative, was a strong factor promoting integration in these reconstituted families. However, if both the husband and wife were employed, the reconstituted family had higher integration if the husband and wife were on equal prestige levels. From this it can be inferred that if the wife did work, her prestige in the job market became significant in the family. There appeared to be less family harmony if either one of the couple was on a higher occupational level, and greater family harmony if the husband was on a higher educational level.

SUMMARY

In summary, the data presented in this chapter indicate that the degree of integration was higher for younger couples than for older couples. Catholic husbands and Protestant wives rated integration in their families higher than did other religious groups, although there was only a slight difference between Catholics and Protestants for either men or women. The integration ratings by Jews and non-affiliates were, however, considerably lower for both sexes, although no conclusions can be drawn because there were too few cases. A difference in religion did not seem to have any effect, nor did educational level.

In those cases where death of a partner had terminated the previous marriage, there were considerably higher integration scores than for those who had been divorced or had never been married before. Integration was greater in those families where there was a child or children from the present marriage.

The findings on the relationship between FIS and social class are not clear, although the working-class families seem to have achieved the highest integration and the middle-class families the lowest. Integration was higher when there was a difference between the husband and wife in educational levels. When both parents worked, integration was higher when there was no difference between them in occupational status, but integration was highest of all when the wife was not working outside the home.

4/The husband-wife relationship

In the previous chapter, the effects of certain variables on the integration of the reconstituted family were discussed. These included the ages of the marital couple, religion and educational levels, previous marital status, the length of the previous marriages, the presence or absence of children from the present marriage, and social class. Now one of the major variables will be examined: the relationship between the husband and the wife.

First, this relationship will be looked at to see which factors may have an effect on it. Then, its effect on the integration of the family will be ascertained. In short, two things about men and women who remarry will be examined: How do their personal relationships compare to those in "once-married" marriages? and, How does their relationship affect the integration of the entire reconstituted family?

HUSBAND-WIFE RELATIONSHIP SCORE

Every couple was given a Husband-Wife Relationship

Score (HWRS) which was calculated in the following way. Each husband and each wife was asked to rate the quality of his or her marital relationship on a continuum from "Very unhappy" to "Very happy." The subjects were also asked, in the written section of the interview, to state their personal feelings about each other.

Each relationship was also rated by the investigator, who based the rating on discussions with each spouse. These five scores were then treated as subscores and combined into a Husband-Wife Relationship Score (HWRS), categorized into "Poor," "Good," and "Excellent." It should be noted that in this HWRS self-ratings were counted twice, as the scores given on the continuum and the scores given in the forced-choice scale are both self-rated scores.

This heavy weighting of "self" scores was desirable for two reasons. One, it was felt that good relationships are more difficult to detect than poor ones, and two, "the privacy of the marital relationship prevents outsiders from judging how 'truly happy' a particular union might be."[1]

TABLE 4.1

Couples' Written Self-Ratings of
Their Marital Relationship

	Husband		Wife	
Rating	percent	number	percent	number
Poor	9	(8)	8	(7)
Good	39	(35)	31	(28)
Excellent	52	(45)	61	(53)
Total	100	(88)	100	(88)

TABLE 4.2

Investigator's Ratings of Marital Relationships

	Marriage	
Rating	percent	number
Poor	37	(33)
Good	38	(33)
Excellent	25	(22)

Table 4.1 shows that the difference between the way that husbands and wives rated their marital relationship was al-

most nil. The scores that were rated on the continuum are not given because they are almost identical with those on the forced-choice scale.

Table 4.2 indicates that the investigator was likely to give the marital relationship a lower score than husbands and wives gave to themselves.

TABLE 4.3

Combined Husband-Wife Relationship Score (HWRS)		
	Percent of Marriages	
Rating	percent	number
Poor to good	46	(40)
Excellent	54	(48)

Because there were too few cases in the "Poor" category, it was combined with the "Good" category. Table 4.3 shows the final HWRS's after the five subscores had been combined. Forty-six percent were rated "Poor to good" and 54 percent "Excellent."

Most sociologists score marital happiness or stability by asking the subjects how they rate their marriages. For example, Harvey J. Locke's study of middle-class remarried couples revealed that 90 percent rated their second marriages as "happy;"[2] and seven out of eight of Jessie Bernard's remarried husbands and wives rated their marriages in the same way.[3] The marital relationship scores obtained in this study were more realistic than those in studies where only the self-ratings were reported, because the researcher's observations were included.

The discrepancy between the self-ratings and the investigator's ratings may be due to one or more factors. The subjects may have been attempting to impress the interviewer; the subjects may have been refusing to acknowledge poor relationships; or the investigator may have held different standards from those held by the participants in a marriage. It is also possible that there were clues the investigator was able to pick up of which the couples were unaware. For example, one couple who had each rated their relationship as "Excellent" gave the investigator reasons to rate it lower. When asked what he thought he and his wife disagreed about, the husband spontaneously replied, "Pick a subject!" He then retracted, saying, "No, I don't mean that. We only have average disagreements, like every other couple."

This husband then went on to note that they fought about money; that he liked outdoor activities and she liked indoor activities; that he was interested in politics and she was not; that he selected older people for friends while she preferred younger people; that they enjoyed different types of foods; that she did not like his family; and that he preferred the mountains for a vacation while she preferred the seashore.

Another couple who were given a lower score by the investigator than the one they had given to themselves were twenty-three years apart in age. The younger wife had never been married before, and the couple had a child from this marriage. The wife seemed totally unaware of the problems the child had created for her husband. She said, "The baby has made a big change in our lives. He waited a long time for his little boy. It was like a miracle to him." The husband, on the other hand, remarked, "It's been very difficult. My age has much to do with it. We have younger friends, which took a lot of adjusting on my part. I had trouble at first because of the baby, at my age, but I am trying to adjust to that too."

A final example concerns a husband who was unaware of some of his wife's problems. He mentioned that their sexual life was fine; the wife said it was very poor, so poor in fact, that she refused to discuss it with the interviewer. The husband felt that at the beginning his wife had been jealous of his first wife and had transmitted her hostility to his children, but he believed the problem had been resolved: "I don't think there is any tension between my kids and my wife any more." The wife, on the other hand, acknowledged that she disliked her stepchildren, especially the younger daughter: "I don't like her because she's not my child. I'm trying to like her for Don's sake and for her sake, too."

These, then, are examples of the kinds of marriages which were rated differently by the marital couple and by the investigator. The difference may be accounted for by the fact that the couples seemed unaware of some deep problem, which was revealed during the interview but which did not seem to occur to them when they were asked to rate their relationship. On the other hand, the subjects may simply have been concealing problems.

CHANGE IN MARITAL RELATIONSHIP

The previous section shows how the couples rated their marital relationship. I was also interested in learning what changes had occurred. The subjects were asked if they thought their relationships with their mates had gotten worse, stayed the same, or improved over the period of the marriage. The table below records their answers.

TABLE 4.4

	Husbands		Wives	
Direction of Change in the Remarriage				
Direction	percent	number	percent	number
Worse or same	30	(24)	32	(25)
Better	70	(55)	68	(53)
Total	100	(79)*	100	(78)*

*Nine men and 10 women could not identify the direction of change in their marriage.

The categories "Worse" and "Same" were collapsed because of the paucity of cases in the "Worse" category. Table 4.4 shows remarkable agreement between husbands and wives on the direction their marriages are taking.

Most of the couples were very much aware of the state of their relationships, which may account for the agreement noted above. One husband phrased it thus:

> Our marriage is great. We don't argue very often; we come to mutual conclusions on just about everything. . . . The marriage is better because we've gone into more areas. We know more about each other; but it was good to start with, so I would say it expanded rather than it got better.

Another husband noted:

> We don't disagree on any topics I can think of. It gets better and better. Instead of shooting broadside at everything, we know what we want, and the more we know each other the more we can zero in on what we want. I think we have a perfect fit. We really think alike.

One wife, who had described her marriage as very

happy and productive and who was very involved with helping her own and her husband's children adjust to life in a well-regulated household, said:

> I really never stop to think if my marriage is getting better or worse. I just go from day to day dealing with the daily problems. With all these kids, there are daily problems, although nothing momentous.

PROBLEM AREAS

Most of the remarried couples, then, recognized that they had good marriages, and generally they were appreciative of their good relationships. This is not to say, however, that they did not have problems or that they were unaware of the problem areas. When asked about such issues, most of the couples, especially those with good relationships, suggested that their disagreements were no different from those in any primary marriage. Table 4.5 shows the areas of conflict which the subjects considered major.

TABLE 4.5

	Major Problems			
	Husbands		Wives	
Problem	percent	number	percent	number
Child-rearing	35	(31)	35	(31)
Money	20	(18)	16	(14)
Sex relations	11	(10)	6	(6)
Religion	10	(9)	6	(5)
Political differences	9	(8)	11	(10)
Outsiders	9	(8)	14	(12)
Recreation	6	(4)	11	(10)
Total	100	(88)	100	(88)

Most of the problems the remarried couples had were the same as cited in the literature for primary marriages, although the order was reversed for the first two problems: child-rearing and money. In their study of husbands and wives, Blood and Wolfe[4] found that money was the major area of disagreement, followed by child-rearing. The finding of this study, however, was to be expected because in reconstituted families children are brought together from homes which may have somewhat different standards and values. Apparently, when a couple cannot resolve their differences of opinion in child-rearing practices, the problem can become quite serious. One wife stated:

> There are problems which come because they aren't his children. Sometimes I think we can't be happy because of this. Sex is not as happy as it should be; but here again, everything is based on the kids. The tension we have is centered on the kids and sometimes it carries over into the bed. You can't go to bed mad and expect to be loving, expecially for a woman.

Her husband agreed with her:

> The children are the biggest problem. They're not mine. I have my ways about how I think they should be raised and of course she doesn't agree. I just hope it won't affect us too much after the raising of the kids is over.

Another wife said:

> There's a lot of tension caused by difference of personality and acceptance. I don't think our marriage is as secure as it should be. Our insecurity comes because of the children. We always had different ideas about bringing up children. I don't think the problem about the kids is going to be solved. I just think they're going to grow up and go away.

This wife's husband seemed to agree with her:

> My marriage isn't too good. I think it may improve when the kids get out, not until. The kids are the big thing. I don't know if we're going to make a go of it. The whole thing hinges on the kids. It will make a vast difference when the kids are out of the house; but there will always be resentment between us.

Thus, children appear to be the biggest problem in re-marriages where there are children from former marriages. When the problem is a major one, it is likely to have vast ramifications. This will be discussed in a later chapter.

None of the problems mentioned by the subjects were surprising because they were the problems commonly found in any marriage. The only finding that differed from any study of marriage was, as mentioned, the reversed order of child-rearing and financial problems.

THE HUSBAND-WIFE RELATIONSHIP AS A DEPENDENT VARIABLE

Of the multitude of factors which could affect the relationship between a husband and a wife, the following were selected: the educational level of the man and the woman; the age of each; their religions; the length of their previous marriages; their previous marital status; the sex of their children and the present residence of their children; and their socioeconomic status.

Education

The findings indicate that of those husbands who had never attended college, 40 percent were in families who had received a HWRS of "Excellent," while 65 percent of those who had gone to college were in "Excellent" rated families. Of the wives without college experience, 54 percent were in the "Excellent" category, compared to 56 percent of those who had gone to college. The conclusion drawn was that if the husband had at least some college, he was more likely to have a more successful relationship with his second wife. The wife's education, on the other hand, did not seem to be of any consequence.

Given the assumption that reconstituted families do not differ in any important ways from primary families, it was expected that high education and marital success would be related. The relationship for primary families is well documented: better educated people have more satisfactory marital relationships.[5] However, this expectation was realized for the remarried husbands, but not for the wives in this study. Goode found in his study of divorced women that the college-educated remarried wives were slightly less satisfied with their second marriages than those with high school or less education. While this is helpful in explaining the current findings, it is not sufficient, because Goode did not compare his responses with a male population, and, furthermore, he noted that his sample was too small to be considered reliable.[6]

The data were examined to see if difference in educational levels between husbands and wives had an effect on their relationships. This was found not to be a factor, contrary to Blood and Wolfe's findings.[7]

Age

Most studies show that youthful marriage is associated with marital failure.[8] Not only is the likelihood of divorce greater among those who marry under twenty years of age, but the trend is consistent for every age; the older the couple, the greater the probability of marital success.[9]

None of the subjects in this study were under twenty years of age at the time of the remarriage. In general, of course, remarriages involve older persons. Jessie Bernard, for example, found that the average age of divorced men at the time of remarriage was 36.8 years and the average for women was 33.7 years. She found that widowed men remarried at the average age of 45.4 and widowed women at 41.0 years of age.[10] In this sample, the mean age for men was 35 years and for women 34.6 years. In remarriage the problem of extreme youth does not often arise. Age was not a factor in the Husband-Wife Relationship Score (HWRS).

Religion

"It has been shown that divorce rates tend to be lowest in Catholic-Catholic marriages, slightly higher in homogamous Jewish and Protestant marriages, and still higher in varying degrees for different types of cross-religious marriages."[11] This common finding is generally explained by the fact that the Catholic church does not recognize divorce. This study, however, found that there was no difference in marital satisfaction among religious groups. The Catholic factor was not operative probably because most of the subjects in the sample has already been divorced and in many cases were nonpracticing Catholics.

In the present study no difference between Protestant and Catholic husbands and wives was found. There were too few cases in the Jewish and unaffiliated categories to warrant consideration. These findings of no difference are in accord with Goode's finding that religion does not play an important role in the success or failure of remarriage.[12]

Twenty-three percent of the marriages in this sample were interfaith marriages. Examination revealed that of those couples who were of the same religion, 59 percent had "Excellent" relationships, compared to 40 percent of those couples who were of different faiths.

Judson T. Landis has shown that interfaith marriages are more likely to end in divorce than intrafaith marriages.[13] While other authors have not concurred in these findings,[14] the prevailing view among family sociologists is that interfaith marriage is less conducive to stability than intrafaith marriage. This was the finding in this study. Religious difference probably negatively influenced marital compatibility in both primary and reconstituted marriages.

Previous marital status

It was found that the length of the previous marriage was not a factor in the stability of the relationship of the remarried couple. However, previous marital status—divorce, death, or never having been married before—did seem to play a role in the current marital relationship.

Of those remarried people whose previous marriages were terminated by death, 71 percent were rated "Excellent" in their current marital relationship. This compares to 51 percent of the divorced and 46 percent of those who had not been married before. The difference betweeen husbands and wives was negligible.

Other investigators have found marital success to be greater among the widowed than among the divorced. Locke,[15] for example, noted that 54 percent of his divorced remarried men and 50 percent of his divorced remarried women had marriages rated "Happy" or "Very happy" compared to 61 percent of the remarried widowers and 64 percent of the remarried widows. The findings of this study were similar to these.

Remarriage has different meanings for those who lost a spouse through divorce than for those who were widowed. Divorce is still somewhat stigmatized in this country,[16] although increasingly less so, and therefore, it is likely that the desire to remarry is stronger for the divorced than it is for the widowed. That marriages between divorced people tend to be less successful than those between widowed people is probably a result of this difference in meaning. Divorced people tend to marry sooner after the termination of the prior marriage than widowed people. There are several reasons for this haste. The widowed and the divorced are treated differently in our society.[17] One point of ambiguity centers around the readmission of divorced people into the social network. In our society there is so much stress on the nuclear family that the divorced are in limbo. We lack precise norms as to their placement. The role of widowed is a respectable one, while that of divorced is more suspect and ambiguous. The divorced person seeks to escape from an uncomfortable social position, while the widowed feels no such necessity. Furthermore, remarriage allows the divorced person to regain feelings of self-worth and provides him or her with an opportunity to prove himself or herself to be a successfully married person. The widowed person needs no such opportunity because he or she does not feel like a failure and is not treated as such by society.

There are other reasons for a shorter interval between marriages among divorced people. One is the fact that divorced men and women generally are younger than the widowed.[18] Furthermore, there is a shorter "mourning" period for the divorced and a greater possibility that the subsequent spouse had been selected before the divorce occurred.[19] In addition, because they are younger, divorced people usually have young children for whom they may be anxious to provide a surrogate parent.

For all these reasons, divorced people tend to remarry more quickly than widowed people. Therefore, there may be less careful consideration given to the selection of a new partner. The result may be that the relationship between the husband and wife may not be as well stabilized as it is among remarried widowed people, who have married under less pressure and who therefore have given more thoughtful reflection to the choice of a second mate.

Children

No relationship was found between the ages and sex of the children and the husband-wife relationship. Neither was a relationship found between the childrens' residence and the HWRS.

Social class

Of the seventeen couples in the working class, 41 percent received "Excellent" ratings on their marital relationship, compared to 54 percent of the forty-eight families in the middle class, and 65 percent of the twenty-three couples in the upper middle class.

There is, then, a moderate relationship between marital success and social class. The higher the social class, the higher the rating for husband-wife relationship. Studies have shown that good marital adjustment increases with social status.[20] Although the present study does not yield a strong relationship, the trend is in the same direction.

FAMILY INTEGRATION AND HUSBAND-WIFE RELATIONSHIP

It was expected that family integration in reconstituted families would not differ greatly from integration in primary families and would be dependent, at least in part, on the relationship between the husband and wife. It would also be dependent on the relationship between the stepparents and the stepchildren; on the relationships of the stepchildren; on the reactions of friends and families; and on social-class position. First, however, what were the effects on family integration of the relationship between the husband and the wife?

TABLE 4.6

	Family Integration							
	Low		Moderate		High		Total	
HWRS	%	#	%	#	%	#	%	#
Poor to good	35	(14)	48	(19)	17	(7)	100	(40)
Excellent	10	(5)	23	(11)	67	(32)	100	(48)

HWRS and Family Integration

Note: G = .7
  r = .527
  r² = .27

Table 4.6 indicates that there is a strong, consistent relationship between family integration and the relationship of the husband and wife.

This finding had been predicted by many sociologists. Adams and Wierath commented, "The heart of the

American family is the marital relationship itself."[21] Because of the great value which Americans place on the husband-wife relationship, the success of this relationship is believed to determine family stability. There was no reason to expect that the stability of a reconstituted family would not be as dependent on the relationship between the husband and the wife as that of a primary family.

SUMMARY

In this chapter, how the Husband-Wife Relationship Score was obtained was described. The final index, composed of two self-ratings by the husband and wife and an evaluation by the investigator, was almost identical with the ratings given by the husbands. Forty-six percent of the couples received a "Poor to good" rating and 54 percent an "Excellent" rating. Approximately 70 percent of the couples believed their relationships were improving. The problems most frequently cited were child-rearing and money, in that order.

The husband and wife relationship was first considered for its own sake. It was found that the higher the educational level of the husband, the greater the probability of an "Excellent" marital relationship. It was found that neither age nor religion were factors in this relationship, although a greater percentage of couples with the same religion were rated "Excellent." It was also found that the ages and sex of the stepchildren and their place of residence were not influences on this relationship. Furthermore, there was a higher percentage of people in the "Excellent" category who had been widowed previously, as opposed to those either divorced or those who had never been married before. Finally, it was determined that the higher the social class position, the greater the probability of high scores on the HWRS scale.

Finally, it was found that the husband-wife relationship was a strong influence on the integration of the reconstituted family. When the husband and wife had a "Poor to good" relationship, the family's integration was likely to be "Low;" when they had an "Excellent" relationship, integration was likely to be "High." This confirms the finding in primary families. Family solidarity is in a large measure dependent on the relationship between the husband and the wife.

5/Stepparent-stepchild relationships

"There is a dearth of research concerning the attitudes of stepparents toward children, the attitudes of children toward stepparents, and the communication patterns between children and stepparents."[1] One study of this relationship[2] contends that regardless of the desire and skill of the stepparent, success is not likely because our social norms make it impossible for him or her to completely take on the parent role.[3] According to most of the writers in this area, this is especially true when there has been a divorce. But even in the case of widowhood, the child is likely to maintain a relationship with the deceased biological parent and, therefore, the stepparent can never totally assume the position of parent.

The "step" relationships will be treated herein as a whole, not as individual relationships. In other words, the constellation of step-relationships will be considered as an entity. Included in the evaluation of any given family are the opinions of both the stepparents and the parents as to the quality of the relationships. As in the situation of the husband and wife relationship, the Parent-Child Relationship Score (PCRS) will first be examined to see which variables affect it. The variables are: the ages, educational levels, religions, and previous marital statuses of the couple; social class; whether or not there are children from the remarriage; the age and sex of the oldest child of each spouse from the former marriage; the residence of the children from the prior marriage; and the husband-wife relationship. Then the effects of the stepparent-stepchild relationships on the family's integration will be considered.

PARENT-CHILD RELATIONSHIP SCORE

The PCRS was obtained in the following way: Each stepparent was asked to rate his or her relationship with each stepchild. Each spouse was asked to evaluate each of his or her own children's relationship with the stepparent. These two ratings produced an index of self-rated step-relations. In addition, the investigator evaluated the relationships, basing the score on the comments of the parents and stepparents in the oral section of the interview and on observation, when possible, of the interaction between the stepchild and the stepparent. Finally, the self-ratings and the investigator's ratings were combined into a final index of stepparent-stepchild relationships.

TABLE 5.1

Self-Ratings by Husbands and Wives
of Their Relationships with
Their Stepchildren

	PCRS						
	Poor		Good		Excellent		Total
	%	#	%	#	%	#	
Husbands	7	(4)	22	(14)	71	(45)	63*
Wives	19	(13)	28	(20)	53	(37)	70*

*Twenty-two of the husbands had no stepchildren and 16 of the wives had no stepchildren. Three of the husbands and 2 of the wives never saw their stepchildren.

Table 5.2 shows that the investigator tended to give both the husbands and the wives a low PCRS. The trend, how-

49

ever, is in the same direction as the self-ratings, with the husbands scoring higher than the wives in their relationships with their stepchildren.

TABLE 5.2

Evaluation by Investigator of the
Relationships Between the
Stepparents and the
Stepchildren

	PCRS						Total
	Poor		Good		Excellent		
	%	#	%	#	%	#	
Husbands	29	(18)	35	(22)	35	(23)	63
Wives	40	(28)	33	(23)	27	(19)	70

TABLE 5.3

Combined Parent-Child Relationships Score

	Relationship Score	
Rating	percent	number
Poor	18	(16)
Good	18	(16)
Excellent	64	(56)
Total	100	(88)

Table 5.3 reveals that when the scores were combined, 64 percent of the families received "Excellent" ratings and 18 percent received "Good" and "Poor" ratings.

The findings suggest that the stepfather was more likely to establish and maintain a good relationship with his stepchild than the stepmother. The most likely reason why stepmothers experienced more difficulty with stepchildren is that they normally spent more time with the children than did fathers and stepfathers, allowing more opportunity for disharmony because of proximity and the nature of the role. Leonard Benson notes that this situation can be attributed to the type of role the father plays, inasmuch as his role is more passive than that of the mother, because his major function is implied in the symbolism of his presence.[4] Bowerman and Irish found that the role of stepmother is indeed more difficult than that of stepfather.[5] Two reasons for this, these authors believe, are that society is more apt to give assistance to the male stepparent, and men are more likely to find social acceptance in the role. Another reason is the myths in various cultures which denigrate the stepmother—the folklore of the cruel and heartless stepmother.[6]

For either sex, the role of stepparent has never been considered an easy one and, therefore, the finding in this study that 64 percent of the families had "Excellent" relationships was a somewhat surprising one. It was not expected that the percentage in this category would be as high as it was.

Many investigators have commented on the difficulties of the step-relationship. William C. Smith repeatedly notes that the relationships between stepchildren and stepparents is considerably less harmonious than between children and parents in primary homes.[7] This author feels that many of the problems are generated by the Cinderella myth, and that the myth does not square with the facts. Bowerman and Irish find that the relationships between stepparents and stepchildren "are marked by greater levels of uncertainty of feelings, insecurity of position, and strain than are those to be found in normal homes."[8]

Margaret Mead offers a possible reason for the general finding that step-relations are not satisfactory. She suggests that in our family system the child develops an overdependence on the parents. This results in a demand on the parents to supply the only possible security for the child. "Each American child learns early and in terror that his whole security depends on that single set of parents. . . . We have never made adequate social provision for the security and identity of the children if that marriage is broken."[9] The result, Mead points out, is an inability of a child to commit himself to a stepparent in a manner that will permit a meaningful relationship.

Paul Bohannan[10] feels that kinship terms in the American culture are inadequate. "Stepparent" was a useful term when death was the usual precursor of remarriage, because the stepparent was a *replacement*. But a stepparent after divorce is an *additional parent*, not a replacement. Stepparents are not real in American culture. The norm is either to ignore the relationship or to take special care to avoid any appearance of difference between parent and stepparent. Our culture does not provide us with norms to show the difference, nor do we have norms for behavior and for expectations. Thus, Bohannan tells us, the creation of a stepparent-stepchild relationship is difficult in our society.

It is apparent, then, that the findings of this study are somewhat opposed to those of other investigators, although the difference is not great. There is some agreement with other work. A study conducted by F. Ivan Nye revealed little evidence to support the notion that there were special problems between stepparents and stepchildren.[11] His data show that although there are more adjustment problems in reconstituted families than there are in intact happy families, the greatest adjustment is needed in intact unhappy primary families. The majority of Goode's remarried mothers thought their children's lives had improved when they remarried.[12] Lee Burchinal's study revealed that the commonly held belief that divorce and remarriage have detrimental effects on the children is erroneous.[13]

Jessie Bernard reported in a study of graduate students who were stepchildren that none of these students differed in terms of stability, self-sufficiency, or dominance from other children in the general college population.[14] This study contained comments of the students concerning the love, help, friendship, and understanding their stepparents had provided, which contradicted the stepparent stereotype.

The stepparents in this study had a great deal to say about their relationships with their spouses' children. Some comments revealed extreme viewpoints. One previously divorced mother noted:

> Here's something strange. With my other friends who are like us, the father loves his own children more than [his wife's]. But it's the opposite with my husband, who loves my girls best. Well, I don't think he loves them more than our son, but he takes more [interest] in them.

Many stepparents did not distinguish between their stepchildren and their own children. One stepmother married to a widower remarked:

> She [the stepdaughter] thinks of me as "mommie." She has called me "mommie" since

Harry and I started going together. It has worked out fine. I'm her mother legally and emotionally, on her part and mine.

The stepfather of boys whose natural father lived nearby said:

I really feel like their father. I want things for them—more, I think, than they realize. They feel like my kids. The real problem is their father being so close. I sometimes wish he would disappear so I could take over. I guess most of the problems between us are the same as any father with his kids. They're not mine so it's hard to say. They raise Cain once in a while, but I think they appreciate what I'm trying to do for them. Makes you feel kinda good.

Another stepfather, whose stepchildren's real father was dead, commented:

They are all my children. It makes no difference to me. My stepchildren don't have a father and I think [being a father] is my job.

One wife spoke of her husband's relationship with her own child:

He's always referred to [my daughter] as his daughter rather than as his stepdaughter. He never made any issue of her being a stepchild. There are times when I think she is closer to him than she is to me. He is more her father than her real father ever was or is now.

There are, of course, those stepparents who were not as successful as the ones quoted above. Nevertheless, the relationships were improving. Among these stepparents there was often a great deal of self-conscious effort made to bring these relationships closer. One husband noted:

At first I didn't feel the closeness to my wife's

daughter [that I would toward] my own child. I'm still conscious of the fact that she isn't mine and I try to overcompensate for it. I try to be a loving father to her.

Another husband said:

There may be some animosity between my daughter and my wife because of me. She wanted me to marry her mommy again. But my daughter tries, I think. It's improving.

One father remarked:

There is some parental feeling, but I think my wife could be more of a parent. Sometimes I think she is a little hard on my daughter and shows favoritism [toward] her own kids.

A smaller group of stepparents were dissatisfied with the relationships, sometimes blaming themselves, sometimes their spouses, and sometimes the children.

I'm satisfied with my wife's treatment of my children, but not of their treatment of her. My children have never accepted Gloria, and they have expressed their hostility in many ways.

My girl and my wife are very distant. She is jealous of her father for marrying another woman. She only lives with us because it is more convenient to live here. I don't blame my wife for any of this.

I think my husband was jealous of my daughter from the day we got married. She now lives with her dad because she was a nervous wreck. She was party to things she never should have been and she heard things a girl her age should never have heard.

Finally, there is simple indifference. One stepfather said:

There isn't much of a relationship between her kids and me . . . probably to avoid conflict.

CHANGE IN THE STEPPARENT-STEPCHILD RELATIONSHIP

In addition to my interest in the present state of the relationship between stepparents and their stepchildren, I was concerned with the changes in that relationship during the period of the remarriage. Therefore, the subjects were asked whether they believed that, in general, the relationships had worsened, stayed the same, or improved over time. Table 5.4 gives the results.

TABLE 5.4

Direction of Change in PCRS					
	Direction of Change				
	Worse or the same		Better		Total
	percent	number	percent	number	percent	number
Husbands	51	(36)	49	(35)	100	(71)*
Wives	53	(40)	47	(35)	100	(75)*

*Nine husbands and 11 wives did not respond to the question. Eight husbands and 21 wives replied that change varied according to individual children.

As we can see from the table, slightly less than one-half of all the subjects felt that relationships between stepparents and stepchildren had improved.

PARENT-CHILD RELATIONSHIP SCORE AS A DEPENDENT VARIABLE

Stepparents' ages

The stepfather's age was not a factor in his relationship with his stepchildren. However, of those stepmothers who were over forty, only 52 percent were rated in the "Excellent" category, compared to 70 percent of those under forty. (The trend was similar for stepfathers, but was not statistically significant.)

Stepparents' educational levels

No difference was found among categories of stepparents' educational levels in their relationships with the stepchildren.

Stepparents' religion

The data show that there is a difference among stepparents in their relationships with their stepchildren in terms of religion, with Protestants scoring higher than Catholics, Jews, or unaffiliates. Seventy-two percent of the Protestant stepparents were in the "Excellent" category, compared to 55 percent of the Catholics, 60 percent of the Jews, and only 47 percent of the unaffiliated. Given the small number of cases in the Jewish and unaffiliated groups, it is not possible to compare them in a meaningful way with the other religious groups. Protestants, both stepfathers and stepmothers, appeared to have better relationships with stepchildren than Catholics, This may be a reflection of the fact that, even if Catholics are inactive, they retain a feeling of guilt about remarriage, which impairs their relations with their stepchildren.

Prior Marital Status

TABLE 5.5

Previous Marital Status of Stepfathers and PCRS

Previous marital status	Poor to good		Excellent		Total	
	percent	number	percent	number	percent	number
Divorce	46	(25)	54	(29)	100	(54)
Death	24	(5)	76	(16)	100	(21)
Never married before	15	(2)	85	(11)	100	(13)

Note: G = .51

The type of termination of the previous marriage was not an influence on the relationship between the stepmother and her stepchildren. However, as revealed in Table 5.5, men who had never been married before had the best relationships with stepchildren, while those who had been divorced had the worst.

Bowerman and Irish[15] obtained the opposite finding and suggested that children of divorced, remarried parents adjust better to the new stepparent because the children tend to be younger and the marriages occur after a shorter time span than for widowed parents. Furthermore, they state, the tension produced by the divorce may cause the children to more readily reject the real parent and accept the stepparent. Other writers[16] have agreed with this view, suggesting that when a parent dies he is likely to gain esteem and respect; when there is a divorce, prestige is frequently lost, thus leaving room for the new stepparent. In addition, visitation of the absent parent may exert an influence on the new relationship. The data in the present study, however, do not reveal any difference between those families in which there was frequent visitation with the biological parent and those in which there was little or none at all.

Social Class

There seems to be a slight direct correspondence between social class and the quality of the stepparent-stepchild relationship, although this correspondence was not as strong as was expected. Seventy percent of those in the upper middle class were rated "Excellent" in the PCRS compared to 62 percent of those in the middle class and 59 percent of those in the working class. Other investigators have also found this weak relationship. Langner and Michael discovered that 20 percent of their higher social class stepchildren reported "Poor" relationships with stepparents compared to 31 percent of the lower class stepchildren.[17] Bell writes, "There *may* also be a social class difference related to children and their getting along with stepparents."[18]

Ages and sex of stepchildren

The oldest child in each family was used to estimate which categories of sex and age would affect the stepparent-stepchild relationship, on the theory that the oldest child influences the attitudes and behaviors of younger children. The sex of the child was not a meaningful factor for either stepparent, nor was age a factor in the stepfather's relationship with his stepchild. However, as Table 5.6 reveals, age was a decided factor for stepmothers.

TABLE 5.6

Ages of stepchildren	PCRS					
	Poor to good		Excellent		Total*	
	percent	number	percent	number	percent	number
Under 13	25	(10)	75	(30)	100	(40)
13 and over	53	(17)	47	(15)	100	(32)

Note: Q = .54
*Sixteen women had no stepchildren.

Stepmothers are more likely to have good relationships with younger stepchildren, whether they are boys or girls, than they are with older stepchildren. Bell,[19] Bernard,[20] and Cavan[21] all corroborate this finding.

These data might be explained in terms of the stepchildren themselves. The younger child is more apt to be trustful and accepting than the older child, who must sever bonds of loyalty to the absent parent. Furthermore, in the United States, children over thirteen are normally rebellious even in primary families; adolescents are generally less likely to be on friendly terms with parents, whether natural or step.[22] In addition, the older child has already adjusted to his or her own parent and is apt to be somewhat set in his ways. With the advent of a stepparent, the child must readjust to accommodate the new relationship and this may be more difficult for the older child than for the younger one. In all events, the stepmother would be the one more likely to be affected because of her more frequent contact with the children.

The subjects in this study were quite divided on the issue of preferable age in stepchildren.[23] One stepfather of older children said, when asked what advice he would give to someone about to remarry:

> If there were young children involved I would say be very hesitant about it. The ideal situation is when the kids are out of the nest.

The stepmother of a three-year-old boy advised:

> If the child is young and you can raise him like your own, go ahead. If the child is older, just try to love him as much as you can.

Another stepmother of young children noted:

> If you have to take on children, take them from three years old on down. It's much safer. I think the younger you get them, the more you can change hostilities.

The three stepparents quoted above all seemed to think

their own situations were preferable. Others felt differently. One stepmother said:

> I think my problems were because the children were so old. If [the children had been younger], I don't think it would have been so difficult.

One wife who had anticipated difficulties for her new husband because her children were teen-agers explained:

> You must be very careful when you make the decision to remarry when you have teen-age children. Children of this age can be very sarcastic, know-it-all, very expensive. Smaller children are more pliable; it's a lot easier. After twelve, you must be careful.

Another stepmother recognized that her problems with teen-aged stepsons were not unique:

> My stepsons are very affectionate toward me. They accept advice except perhaps the usual fourteen- and fifteen-year-old know-it-all.

One mother was very alert to her son's problem:

> My older boy had a problem with my second husband because he switched his affections from his real father to my husband. He felt guilty about it.

The widowed father of seven summed up the differences age makes when he commented:

> My oldest children can't totally accept my wife as mother. My nineteen-year-old girl and my wife don't really like each other, but my wife tries. My seventeen-year-old has improved since the two older children left. The fourteen-year-old and the two youngest ones tend to accept my wife as a mother.

It can be seen from the above quotations that several

people in this sample felt that remarriage and the establishment of a reconstituted family is easier when the stepchildren are young.

Residence of children from former marriages

TABLE 5.7

Residence of Mothers' Children from Former Marriages and PCRS					
	PCRS				
Children's residence	Poor to good		Excellent		Total*	
	percent	number	percent	number	percent	number
At home	33	(19)	67	(40)	100	(59)
Away	56	(4)	44	(3)	100	(7)

Note: Q = .47
*Twenty-two of the mothers did not have children from former marriages.

Investigation indicated that the stepfather's parental feelings for his stepchildren were not influenced by the residence of his own children. The situation, however, was quite different for stepmothers, as shown in Table 5.7. However, the finding is not reliable given the fact that there were only seven women in the sample whose children did not live with them.

Most of the seven mothers in this sample did not discuss reasons why their children were living with their former husbands or, in rare cases, with grandparents. In one case the mother explained that her daughter lived with her real father because the stepfather was overly jealous and could not tolerate the little girl in his home.

The reason for less amicable relations with stepchildren when the mother's own children did not live with her seems apparent. When the mother does not have custody of her own children, for whatever reasons, it is likely that because of societal norms[24] she will feel guilty about it. Her relationships with her stepchildren, then, are likely to be impaired because she is apt to withhold from them what she may feel she should be giving to her own children.[25] This reasoning is conjectural; there is no evidence in the data to substantiate the investigator's opinions as to why those mothers whose children did not live with them were less able to establish "Excellent" relationships with their stepchildren than those mothers whose children lived with them and fathers in both categories.

Children from present marriage

TABLE 5.8

Children from Present Marriage and PCRS						
	PCRS					
Children from present marriage	Poor to good		Excellent		Total	
	percent	number	percent	number	percent	number
Yes	22	(8)	78	(29)	100	(37)
No	47	(24)	53	(27)	100	(51)

Note: Q = .52

It can be inferred from Table 5.8 that the presence of "new" children in a reconstituted family enhanced the relationships between stepchildren and stepparents. It is probable that when a remarried couple have a child they feel more secure in their relationship. Of course, it is possible that the reverse is also true: Security with each other leads to the likelihood of having a child. However, it is a moot point because probably having a child and feeling secure in the new relationship are two variables that vary directly. If this is true, then such security is apt to result in more comfortable feelings with children from prior marriages. This seems especially likely when one member of the couple has not had a child in a former marriage. In any event, this is speculation, because there is nothing in the data to indicate why having a child improves the step-relationships within the family.

Husband-wife relationship score and PCRS

TABLE 5.9

HWRS and PCRS						
	PCRS					
	Poor to good		Excellent		Total	
HWRS	percent	number	percent	number	percent	number
Poor to good	48	(19)	52	(21)	100	(40)
Excellent	27	(13)	73	(35)	100	(48)

Note: Q = .41
r = .396
r^2 = .15

Table 5.9 shows that of those couples who rated "Poor to good" in their HWRS, 52 percent had "Excellent" relationships with stepchildren; of those with "Excellent" HWRS, 73 percent were also in the "Excellent" PCRS category.

There has been a great deal written about the effect of the husband-wife relationship on children in the primary family. There has also been some attention directed toward the fact that when couples are satisfied in their marital roles, their feelings are reflected in their attitudes and dealings with their children. However, as Robert R. Bell says, "These role questions are only beginning to be adequately researched."[26]

The assumption that reconstituted families do not differ significantly from primary families led to the expectation that the variables HWRS and PCRS would vary directly; that is, if the HWRS score is low, the PCRS will also be low, and vice versa. This correlation should be even stronger in the reconstituted family because the stepchild has no claim on the stepparent's affection. A biological child can legitimately conclude that he or she has an independent relationship with the parent; but the stepchild cannot make the same assumption about the stepparent. Therefore, it is reasonable to suppose that the stepparent's feelings for the stepchild are influenced by the marital relationship. If that relationship is less than desirable, the stepparent is quite likely to withhold or withdraw affection from the stepchild. If the remarriage is successful and the stepparent is satisfied with the marital role and the new spouse, it is likely that there would be a positive influence on the relationship with the stepparent's own children and stepchildren. The table clearly indicates that the PCRS is dependent on the HWRS.

Family Integration and PCRS

TABLE 5.10

	PCRS and Family Integration					
	Family Integration					
	Poor to good		Excellent		Total	
PCRS	percent	number	percent	number	percent	number
Poor to good	84	(27)	16	(5)	100	(32)
Excellent	39	(32)	61	(34)	100	(56)

Note: Q = .7
r = .50
r^2 = .25

It can be seen from Table 5.10 that there is a consistent, clear relationship between the stepparent-stepchildren relationships score and the family integration score. The table indicates that, as had been anticipated, the integration of the reconstituted family is highly dependent on the relationships between the stepparents and the stepchildren. A few of the parents who had an "Excellent" PCRS commented on the integration of their families:

> Our family is extremely close. We love each other and prefer to do things as a unit.

> We do everything together. We're a family. And that's the way it has to be. It can't be yours and mine.

> My girls, our son, me, and my husband are just one group. I never think about us as separate. It never crosses my mind.

> We're all one. Dennis says he has four children. We're very close and do things together.

> When we go out I see all five of us as a total group. We are automatically assumed to be a family of five. It's when we have my girls for weekends that we have this total kind of feeling.

One stepmother who had no children of her own and whose reconstituted family rated a "Good" noted:

> I think if it came right down to someone attacking a member, yes, we would be one unit. We do not do things with the older children. Only my husband, myself, and the youngest girl are really a family.

Two of the stepparents who were in the "Poor" PCRS category commented:

> We don't do anything with his children because they don't want to. Sometimes we do things with my children when they come to visit.

> We don't really do things together. My kids
> weren't [in favor of] my getting married. We
> talked to a social worker a few times, but it didn't
> solve any problems.

SUMMARY

This chapter described the manner in which a Parent-
Child Relationship Score was obtained. Each stepparent was
asked to rate his or her own relationship with each stepchild
and his or her opinion of the spouse's relationship with the
child. The investigator also evaluated these relationships.
The ratings were then combined into a Parent-Child
Relationship Score (PCRS). Eighteen percent of the families
were rated "Poor," another 18 percent were rated "Good,"
and 64 percent received an "Excellent" rating. The findings
indicate that stepfathers are more apt to achieve "Excellent"
ratings on this variable than stepmothers. Slightly less than
one-half of all stepparents believed that there were changes
for the better in their relationships with their stepchildren.

The stepfathers' ages were not found to be influential in
their relationship with their stepchildren. Older stepmothers were less likely to be in the "Excellent" category
than younger stepmothers. Protestants scored higher than
Catholics or Jews or nonaffiliates. Educational level was not a
factor. If the previous marriage was terminated by death
rather than by divorce, the data indicate that sucessfuul step-
relations were more likely to occur for both men and
women. Surprisingly, stepfathers who had never been
married before had the greatest percentage in the
"Excellent" category, while stepmothers in the same position had the smallest percentage in the "Excellent" category.

Social class had small influence in these relationships, al-
though there was some indication that they were related.
The higher the social class, the greater the probability of
"Excellent" stepparent-stepchild relationships.

The data show that the sex of the stepchild was not a factor in these relationships. In addition, age was not an influence for stepfathers, although stepmothers with younger
children scored higher on this variable. The stepfather's
relationship with his stepchildren was not affected by the
place of residence of his own children, while this was an
important factor in the scores for stepmothers. Finally, the

advent of new children decidedly improved the PCRS. As expected, the relationship between the husband and wife greatly influenced the relationship between the stepparent and the stepchildren.

Finally, the PCRS was an important indicator of the integration of the whole family, although it was not as meaningful as the relationship between the husband and wife.

The data show, then, that the stepfather generally had a better relationship with his stepchildren than the stepmother had with her stepchildren. However, the stepmother had a stronger effect on the family's total parent-child scores. Of the seven variables examined (age, religion, reason for termination of prior marriage, educational level of parents, residence of children, ages of children, and sex of children), three affected the PCRS for the stepmother only (age of stepmother, age of stepchild, and residence of her own children). This was expected in view of the fact, as noted early in this chapter, that the stepmother's role is a more active one than the stepfather's, leaving her in a more vulnerable position to incur the affection or the dislike of her stepchildren.

6/Stepsibling relationships

Remarriage creates not only new affinal and parental relationships, but also new sibling affiliations. Often two sets of children, one from the man's former family and one from the woman's, are brought together into the same household. More frequently, however, the father's children are weekly visitors and the mother's children are permanent residents. In either event, these children are suddenly thrust into relationships with each other and are expected to "get along together."

Unfortunately, the relationships of siblings have been neglected by sociologists,[1] so that comparisons between the relations of siblings and stepsiblings cannot be made. Relations among stepsiblings and among half-siblings have been virtually ignored.

The authors who have considered sibling relationships assume a psychological perspective and concentrate on sibling rivalry, birth order, sibling displacement, and the like. Those who do concentrate on the sociological aspects of the sibling relationship usually believe the relationship to be strong, second only to that between parent and child. It has been suggested that "sibling solidarity" may be the "fundamental kinship bond within bilateral systems."[2] Cumming and Schneider found that during some phases of the life cycle, for certain individuals, the tie with siblings was stronger than the tie with spouses.[3]

Several authors have noted the important functions the sibling relationship performs.[4] The possession of a sibling makes the early socialization process more complete because it provides peer role models and training in cooperation, accommodation, and conflict management. Furthermore, siblings offer each other companionship, emotional security, and love. Having a sib means that one learns early how to share privileges and obligations. Finally, the relationship evokes the idea of fair play and provides an early concept of social reality. The probability is high that these positive aspects of intrasib interaction eventually enter the stepsibling relation, although the degree of intensity is probably low.

Some researchers have pointed out the negative aspects of having siblings.[5] Differences in age, sex, and personality structure can partially explain disagreements among brothers and sisters. A sib is often viewed as a rival and a threat; competition is assumed to be natural among siblings. Cliques often form in families, either between a pair of siblings or between one child and one parent, leaving others feeling shut out. The negative aspects are surely present in stepsib relationships also, probably in an exacerbated form.

The stepsibling relationship (SSRS) will be considered first in order to see the effects of the following variables on it: the residence of the children; whether or not there are children from the present marriage; parental educational levels; parental ages; the husband-wife relationship; the stepparent-stepchild relationship; and social class. Age and sex of the children could not be examined because there were too few cases. The effects of the stepsibling relationship on the family's integration will be examined as an independent variable. All correlations are to be viewed with skepticism because of the small number of cases.

STEPSIBLING RELATIONSHIP SCORE

The Stepsibling Relationship Score (SSRS) was obtained by asking each parent to rate his or her child's relationship with each stepsibling on a continuum from one to three. In addition, each parent was asked during the oral part of the interview to evaluate the relationships between the two sets of children. The four scores were combined into a SSRS by adding them together and dividing by four in order to obtain a mean. No evaluation by the investigator was possible because there was no opportunity to observe the children together; nor were the children asked for their opinions or attitudes. Furthermore, because of the small sample, an empirical differentiation could not be made between sets of siblings who lived together and those who did not.

TABLE 6.1

	Stepsibling Relationship Score	
	Relationship Score	
Rating	percent	number
Poor	38	(17)
Good	38	(17)
Excellent	24	(11)
Total	100	(45)

Few of the stepsiblings in this study seemed to have formed meaningful relationships. The comments below are from some of those families with a "Poor" SSRS.

> The twins and my stepdaughter hate each other. The rest of the kids get along all right, but I don't think there's a great deal of love there. They always pull this bit about "your mommie" and "my daddy" jazz. There's lots of jealousy among them. The kids drive us crazy with fighting. I think it has gotten worse.

> The relationship between her children and my children is bad because the hostility from my children, especially my daughter, comes out in many different ways. She resents the fact that my stepdaughters live with me and that she lives in a smaller house and that her mother is difficult, to say the least.

The following remarks were made by those parents who rated the relationships among their children "Good."

At the beginning you would find my husband's four children off playing in one corner and my two playing in another corner. But now they don't do that. There's no open hostility, and we handle it by trying very hard to be fair. Time and adjustment have brought on improvements in the relationships among them all.

There is some rivalry on my daughter's part because she has to share with others and she's not used to that. She really loves them and loves playing with the two younger ones. They intermingle, but the two older ones try to shut my daughter out; maybe that's age though. I think they are closer now.

Those parents who felt that their children had developed "Excellent" relationships made the following statements:

The relationships among the children are great. It's the most marvelous thing because they don't have the grouches that adults have. It's like one family. They're always together. Like most brothers, they fight, but they are wonderful together. It's a beautiful thing. They just never think that they aren't brothers. They have gotten closer and closer.

Our boys are the same age to the day. They act just like brothers. His son and my son are more alike than the two real brothers are. They all refer to each other as brothers; they are like one family.

STEPSIBLING RELATIONSHIP SCORE
AS A DEPENDENT VARIABLE
Change in the stepsibling relationship

Parents were asked to estimate the changes they had observed in their children and stepchildren during the years they had been married. Table 6.2 indicates that almost one-half of the relationships had changed for the better.

TABLE 6.2

Parental Estimation of the Direction
of Change in the Relationships
Between Stepsiblings

Direction	Percent of families	
	percent	number
Worse	16	(7)
Same	42	(19)
Better	42	(19)
Total		(45)

Residence of children

The expectation was that if both sets of children lived in the same household, their relationships with each other would be closer than if one group of children merely visited. This expectation was based partly on George Homans's assumption that "people who interact frequently with one another tend to like one another."[6] Homans qualified this assumption by saying that this is true when interaction is freely chosen and can be discontinued at will. If people are forced to interact, then the probability that they will come to dislike each other is equal to the probability that they will come to like each other.

The paucity of cases precludes drawing any conclusions. Somewhat better relationships were found among stepsibs who live together than among those who do not. Of the twenty-four families with two sets of children living in the home, 29 percent were in the "Excellent" SSRS category compared to 19 percent of the twenty-one families who did not have children living together. One father explained the situation:

> There's rivalry and hostility [between the step-siblings], but it's more dormant now than it has been. There will always be some rivalry. I think it comes about because my daughter doesn't live here and doesn't know what's going on between her father and his stepchildren and is unsure of the position between her and her father.

Children from the new marriage

It was anticipated that when the remarried couple had a child together, the relationships among the children from their former marriages would be closer than in those families where there were no children from the present marriage. This was expected because the new child could serve as a bond between the two groups of children or it could serve to unite them in mutual jealousy. The comments of the respondents seemed to substantiate that a new baby unites the older sets of children. One stepmother put it this way:

> My children and my stepchildren like each other more since we had the baby. They all adore the baby! I don't think the older children are really pals, but at least they have the baby in common.

Of the forty-five couples with families of two sets of siblings from previous marriages, nine couples had children together, 44 percent of whom rated "Excellent" on the SSRS scores. Only 19 percent of the thirty-six couples who did not have children together rated in the same category. It is of interest to note that of the thirty-seven couples in the total sample who had had children together, in only twenty-four percent did both parents have children from previous marriages. Two impressions emerge from these data. One, having children together in a new marriage helps the children from former marriages to form good relationships with each other. Two, when both partners to a remarriage have children from previous marriages, the likelihood is that they will not have children together.

Parental educational level

On the grounds that the more highly educated parents would be more capable of helping their children adjust to each other in a remarriage (because of their greater exposure to media and their greater sensitivity and awareness), it was expected that parents with the highest educational levels would have children with the highest SSRS. Data indicate that this expectation was not realized. Families in which the father had not attended college achieved higher stepsibling relationship scores. Sixteen percent of those who had gone to college were in the "Excellent" category compared to 35 percent of those who had not gone to college. The education of the wife seemed to be of no influence in the relationship between her children and her stepchildren.

Parental age

Young parents were expected to be more likely to have children who got along well together because such parents would be more apt to understand sibling rivalry and jealousy than older parents. Of those husbands who were under forty, 60 percent had "Excellent" SSRS compared to 14 percent of those fathers over forty. Of the mothers under forty, 27 percent had "Excellent" SSRS compared to 22 percent of those over forty. Although age seemed to be an important variable for fathers and an unimportant one for mothers, no definitive statement can be made because there were too few cases.

Husband-wife relationship

TABLE 6.3

	HWRS and SSRS					
	SSRS					
	Poor to good		Excellent		Total	
HWRS	percent	number	percent	number	percent	number
Poor to good	85	(17)	15	(3)	100	(20)
Excellent	68	(17)	32	(8)	100	(25)

Note: Q = .45

The data show that of those families with a "Poor to good" HWRS, only 15 percent were in the "Excellent" SSRS category compared to 32 percent of those in the "Excellent" HWRS category.

Of the total sample, six couples or 7 percent were rated "Poor" in the HWRS. Four of these couples had two sets of children. Of the total sample, thirty-four, or 39 percent, were rated "Good" in the HWRS. Forty-seven percent of them had two sets of children. Of the forty-eight, or 54 percent, who rated "Excellent" in the HWRS, 46 percent had two sets of children. The couples rated "Poor," then, were overrepresented among those families wherein both parents had children from former marriages.

Stepparent and stepchild relationships

It was expected that if the stepparent had formed a good relationship with the stepchild, his or her own child would be more likely to form good relationships with the stepsiblings.

TABLE 6.4

	PCRS and SSRS					
	SSRS					
	Poor to good		Excellent		Total	
PCRS	percent	number	percent	number	percent	number
Poor to good	94	(16)	6	(1)	100	(17)
Excellent	64	(8)	36	(10)	100	(28)

Note: Q = .74

It would seem from the table that the relationship between the two sets of children was somewhat dependent on that between the stepparent and the stepchild. And, when the married couple were getting along well together, their children also seemed to get along well together.

Social class

Social class was expected to affect the PCRS and the HWRS. The higher the social class, the better the relations among stepchildren were expected to be. Of the seventeen couples in the working class in the total sample, 47 percent had two sets of children; of the forty-eight couples in the middle class, 48 percent had two sets of children; and of the twenty-three couples in the upper middle class, 61 percent had two sets of children. Thirty-eight percent of those stepsiblings in the working class had "Excellent" relations compared to 26 percent of those in the middle class and 14 percent of those in the upper middle class.

Although the relationship between the variables was not strong, it was apparent that the lower the social class, the better the relations between stepsiblings. Perhaps this deviation can be understood if we consider that lower-class families, more often than either middle-class or upper-middle-class families, take relatives into their homes on a temporary basis when there are financial or other difficulties. It may be, then, that lower-class children have gotten used to seeing strangers in their homes and are therefore more likely to react positively. This may explain, in part, why the lower-class children seemed to have developed better relationships with stepsiblings than the middle- or upper-middle-class children.

FAMILY INTEGRATION AND SSRS

TABLE 6.5

	SSRS and FIS							
	Family integration							
	Low		Moderate		High		Total	
SSRS	%	#	%	#	%	#	%	#
Poor to good	26	(9)	48	(16)	26	(9)	100	(34)
Excellent	0	(0)	18	(2)	82	(9)	100	(11)

Note: G = .8

It is clear that the relations between sets of stepchildren had an effect on the total family integration. This finding seems logical because when there is friction in one dyad in any group, the entire group will be affected. Therefore, no matter how compatible the parents may be with each other and the stepparents and stepchildren may be with each other, if the stepsiblings themselves are incompatible, the integration of the entire family must be affected.

SUMMARY

In this chapter, it was shown that the Stepsibling Relationship Score (SSRS) was obtained by combining the rating of each parent of his or her own children's relationships with each of his or her stepchildren on a continuum and of his or her opinion of these relationships as told to the investigator. Of the eighty-eight families in the sample, only forty-five contained two sets of children from former marriages. Therefore, any correlations must be considered as tentative. Twenty-four percent of these rated "Excellent" on the SSRS, 38 percent rated "Good," and 38 percent rated "Poor." Forty-two percent of the parents felt the relations between their children had stayed the same, another 42 percent thought they had improved, and 16 percent felt they had worsened.

When both sets of children lived in the same house, the relations between them were more likely to be "Excellent" than if they lived in different houses. Furthermore, when the remarried couple had a child together, their children were likely to have more harmonious relations.

SSRS scores were higher when the father had less education than when he had more; education of the mother was not an influence. Younger stepfathers seemed to have children and stepchildren who got along better than older stepfathers; the age of the stepmother was not a factor. In addition, if the parents had a good relationship, it was likely that the children would also. When the stepparent and stepchildren related well to each other, the children were more apt to do the same. Finally, lower-social-class stepsibs got along better than middle- or upper-middle-class stepsibs. The lower the social class, the better the relations between the two sets of stepsiblings were. As expected, the better the relations between the stepsibs were, the better the total family integration.

Most of the findings in this chapter are difficult to explain. There are two reasons for this. One, the number of families with two sets of stepchildren was too small to give a great deal of credence to the findings. Two, the absence of research on the subject of sibling and stepsibling relationships is a deterent to coherent explanation.

7/Outsiders' attitudes

Family units are embedded in kinship groups and in larger society of which they are a part. Elizabeth Bott's study of twenty London families made clear the probability that the family does not completely determine its own destiny. It is determined partly by the set of social relationships which surround the family.[1] Because they cannot exist in a vacuum, families must consider their relationships with the outside world. The respondents in this study were asked to discuss the attitudes of family, friends, and ex-spouses toward the reconstituted family and to explain whether or not, in their opinion, these attitudes affected the new family.

EX-SPOUSES' ATTITUDES

During the taped part of the interview, the subjects were asked to describe their present relationships with their ex-spouses. Table 7.1 reveals the answers to this question. Then they were asked to evaluate the effects of their relationships on their present marital relations, on their relations with their own and their stepchildren, and on the family as a whole.

TABLE 7.1

| | Relationships with Ex-Spouses | | | |
| | Husbands | | Wives | |
Attitudes	percent	number	percent	number
Negative	41	(22)	29	(15)
Indifferent	43	(23)	59	(30)
Positive	16	(9)	12	(6)
Total	100	(54)*	100	(51)*

*Thirteen of the husbands and 20 of the wives had never been married before. Twenty-one of the husbands and 17 of the wives had been widowed.

"Negative" means that there are feelings of hostility and ill will between the respondent and his or her former spouse. "Positive" attitudes indicate that there is cooperation between them, with some feelings of warmth and sympathy. "Indifference" means that the former mate is regarded as having no significance or value in the present; that the relationship is marked by no special liking for or disliking of the ex-mate. Given the small number of cases, all correlations must be considered with reservations, and no conclusions should be drawn.

The findings in Table 7.1 indicate that the husbands in the sample had more difficulty with their ex-wives than the women in the sample had with their ex-husbands. Furthermore, the men were less likely to be indifferent to their wives.

Jessie Bernard[2] found that 27 percent of the remarried men and 22 percent of the remarried women were friendly toward the divorced spouse compared to 16 percent and 12 percent, respectively, in this sample. Only 19 percent and 27 percent of the men and women in the Bernard study felt unfriendly toward their former spouses, compared to 41 percent of the men in this sample and 29 percent of the women. The majority of Bernard's subjects felt indifference: 54 percent of the men and 51 percent of the women, as did the majority of our subjects. Bernard, however, does not believe that the indifference was real; rather, she feels that there were veiled negative feelings. She points out that indifference toward a former spouse is a socially-imposed attitude. In the present study, the indifference seemed to be valid and no hidden hostility was detected.

William J. Goode, in his study of divorced women, notes that there is an increase in negative feelings toward the ex-husband among women after their remarriage. "These ex-wives have a new or renewed standard of comparison, such that their former husbands appear even less adequate than immediately after the divorce."[3] He also said, "The reconstitution of a full household gives the woman a strong hand in dealing with her ex-husband. . . . The mother is better able to resist the otherwise potential power of the husband to divide the children's loyalties in some substantial manner."[4]

The findings in this study are in accord with Goode's, then, that the wife does not find the ex-husband's influence in her reconstituted family to be of great consequence. Over one-half of our subjects were indifferent to the former husband and only 29 percent believed he had a bad effect on the new family. One mother had this to say:

> The situation [between the wife and her former husband concerning the children] has improved since my second marriage because my former spouse doesn't feel that he can push me around as much. He used to try to get back at me through the children, but he does that less now.

Another remarried mother remarked:

> My ex-husband gave us a lot of grief about visiting the children. Many times he said he was coming and never showed up or called. It's all changed now that I'm married. I think both his marriage and mine have helped to improve the situation.

The husbands, however, felt quite different. It may be that the continuing need to pay alimony to the ex-wife is an irritant when a man has a new family. His resentment of these payments may cause him to make the payments late or to attempt to avoid paying at all. The ex-wife's reaction may be to involve him in legal proceedings which he may see as disruptive to his new life. Thus, the need to continue paying alimony may be seen by the remarried husband as destructive to his remarriage in two ways: if he delays or stops payment, he may have legal problems with his former wife; two, it may be a financial hardship, bringing about a reaction from the present wife. One husband put it this way:

> I think Polly is always aware of her [his former wife]. She sees money go out and we could certainly use it for things around here. So my ex-wife is a factor.

There is another way in which the remarried father may feel his ex-wife is a negative influence in his new marriage. Since it is likely that his visitation with his children and his relationship with them will be, at least partially, dependent on his former wife, she may be obstructive or he may feel that she is. Many ex-wives do make it difficult, if not impossible, for fathers to see their children on a regular basis. Many also try to influence the children against their father and against their stepmother and stepsiblings. These attempts on the part of the ex-wife may indeed cause friction in the new home. Several parents made comments on this kind of situation:

> I see my son very rarely and this is not satisfactory to me. His mother may have been prevailing upon him to stay home. I'm not sure, but I feel something like this.

> At times I feel that we should see them more often than we do. One reason is the problem of making the arrangements, the details of the visit. This always seems to involve some headache—what time, where to take them. We don't see them as often as we are able to or as we should. My first wife doesn't make it any easier.

A third reason why an ex-wife may seem to play a greater role than an ex-husband in a reconstituted family is jealousy on the part of the second wife. One remarried woman made the following remark:

> For a long while his ex-wife wouldn't let the younger girl come over. So I feel hostile toward her and sometimes I'm jealous.

Some fathers felt that the ex-spouse was a factor because after the children visited with their biological mother they could not seem to adjust to returning home again. One father noted:

> I think there are some emotional problems after Laura's mother sees her. She's not the same when she comes home. She's usually very wild and difficult to control. It's hard for her to become a member of the household again.

Another father talked about his daughter's love for his present wife and explained how disruptive such love could be for the child and for the reconstituted family:

> My younger girl has some problems because her real mother keeps calling her up and promising her monetary things if she will come and live with her and all the girl really wants is affection, which my wife gives. So the child is torn between two poles at this point. I think she feels guilty for loving my wife as much, if not more, than her real mother.

There are some fathers who have had so much difficulty with former wives that they have given up entirely:

> My little boy is not allowed to come here. I can't have him in the company of my wife or her children. This is at my ex-wife's request. She's a very hard individual. If I tried to compel her to do this, with an attorney or something, she would do everything in her power to alienate my boy. She's capable of anything and I'm not willing to risk it. I'm hoping in time, and I'm sure it will take a great deal of time, she will allow this.

> His wife wouldn't let him see the kids when it was convenient for him, only when it was convenient for her, so we just agreed that she should keep them.

Finally, as mentioned before, there are those remarriages in which the former spouses have been helpful. One woman stated:

> We [her husband's first wife and herself] get along very well. We're almost friends, I guess because they never hated each other. We meet at family functions. She's really a very wonderful person. I don't mean I pal around with her, but we're on very friendly terms. I think it's unusual. She even likes my baby and plays with him. She's really an awfully broadminded person, and so are her children.

Another stepmother reported that her husband's former wife had voluntarily given up her children to her husband at the time of the divorce because she thought the children were better off with him:

> I've got no problems about her visiting. The kids, even my daughter, call her "other mommie." When she visits she takes my little girl too. For the hours that she visits, she's absolutely great. She can think of more wild things to do and the kids look forward to going with her. She even helped me at first. She would call and give me her ideas about the kids.

EX-SPOUSES' ATTITUDES AS A DEPENDENT VARIABLE

The selected variables which may affect attitudes toward ex-spouses are: the age of the husband and wife; the length of the previous marriage; the religion of the husband and wife; and social class.

Age

It was expected that older people would be more resentful both in terms of the divorce and in terms of the re-marriage of an ex-spouse, and also that older people would be less able to sever past ties, even after remarriage. Therefore, it was anticipated that the older the husband and the wife, the more likely there would be negative feelings from and toward the former spouse.

It was found, however, that age was not a factor in the

attitudes of husbands toward their former wives. Thirty-seven percent of the men under forty and 43 percent of those over forty felt hostility. Forty-seven and 40 percent respectively felt indifference, and 16 and 17 percent respectively felt positive feelings toward their former wives.

However, age was a greater influence for wives. In terms of negative feelings, there appeared to be little difference; 31 percent of wives under forty and 27 percent of those over forty felt their former husbands were hostile to their reconstituted families. Sixty-four percent of the younger wives were indifferent to their former husbands, compared to 46 percent of wives over forty. Finally, only 5 percent of the wives under forty felt positively toward their former spouses, compared to 27 percent of the older wives who felt the same way.

It seems, then, that young wives are more likely to make a greater commitment to the new family. Many more of them are indifferent to their former husbands and fewer of them experience positive feelings than older wives. It appears that older women have more difficulty rebuilding new lives; even though they have remarried, they maintain ties with the former spouse. The expectation was upheld, then, for the wives in the study, but not for the husbands. Older wives are less indifferent to former spouses and receive more positive expression from them.

Length of previous marriage

It was expected that the longer a person had been previously married, the more negative his or her attitude toward an ex-spouse would be. Thirty-four percent of those who had been married ten years or less had negative feelings, compared to 38 percent previously married over ten years. Fifty percent of each category felt indifferent; 16 percent and 12 percent, respectively, had positive feelings. Therefore, length of previous marriage had no bearing on the present attitude toward the ex-spouse. Data also indicate no difference between men and women in this regard.

Religion

The paucity of cases in the Jewish and unaffiliated categories precludes any discussion of them. Therefore, the comparison was confined to Protestants and Catholics. For the remarried couples, religion did not appear to be a factor in their relationships with their former mates. That is, no one religious group was more strongly represented in any of the categories. Thirty-six percent of the Protestants and 39 percent of the Catholics harbored negative feelings. Forty-five percent of the Protestants and 54 percent of the Catholics felt indifference. Nineteen percent of the Protestants and 7 percent of the Catholics believed their feelings were positive. Again, there was no difference between men and women.

Social class

The findings imply that the husband's social class was, by and large, not an important factor influencing his attitude toward his ex-wife, although there was some suggestion that the middle-class men were more likely to have negative feelings and to experience less indifference than men in either of the other two classes. Social class was also not a factor for wives, although working-class wives were heavily represented in the "Indifferent" category (87 percent). Like their husbands, middle-class wives were less indifferent and had more negative feelings than the other classes. Although a trend seems indicated, the fact that there were only nine wives in the working-class category makes it difficult to draw any conclusions. It is possible that middle-class remarried people feel less indifferent and more negative toward their ex-spouses than working-class or upper-middle-class remarried people.

The majority of remarried men and women were indifferent toward former mates, although a higher percentage of men than women experienced negative feelings. The age of the man was not a factor. On the other hand, young wives were more likely than older wives to feel indifference and less likely to have positive feelings. The length of the prior marriage was not an influence for men or women; nor was there any indication that membership in a particular religious group was a factor. Middle-class men and women were apt to feel less indifference and more hostility than either working-class or the upper-middle-class people.

ATTITUDES OF FAMILY AND FRIENDS

David Schneider had discussed the notion that the relative is a person,[5] that is, the determination of who is one's relative is by the perception of the individual, rather than by a fact of biology. Kinship, Schneider says, is based on concern, love, and interest. Therefore, some friendships have the characteristics of kin relations, while some kin relations resemble mere acquaintanceship.

It is for this reason that relatives and close friends were placed in one category when the respondents were asked about attitudes toward their remarriages and reconstituted families. It was felt that if the relationship were close, the relative and the friend could both have the same impact, whether negative or positive.

Couples were asked to describe what they thought the reactions of their friends and families were to their reconstituted families. Given the fact that remarriage, especially when children are involved, is difficult, it was assumed that the attitudes of close associates would affect the remarriage because approval implies support and disapproval implies hindrance.

The category "Indifference" can mean either that there was a total lack of interest on the part of the outsider toward the remarriage, or that no feelings were expressed, or that the couple was not concerned with the attitudes of the outsiders. In any event, the attitudes did not have an effect on the reconstituted family. "Rejection" indicates that the kin group refused to acknowledge or to help the new family in any way. "Acceptance" means that the reconstituted family was considered suitable and was admitted to membership in the kindred.

TABLE 7.2

	Attitudes of Kin as Perceived by Husbands and Wives			
	Husbands		Wives	
Attitude	percent	number	percent	number
Rejection	13	(11)	10	(9)
Indifference	39	(34)	45	(40)
Acceptance	48	(43)	45	(39)
Total	100	(88)	100	(88)

One score for each family on this variable was obtained by averaging the husband's and the wife's scores together.

TABLE 7.3

	Combined Score on Perceived Attitudes of Outsiders (OAS)	
	Families	
Attitude	percent	number
Rejection	13	(11)
Indifference	28	(25)
Acceptance	59	(52)

The finding of Table 7.3 was anticipated because the social expectation in our society is that the adult, both male and female, *should* be married. Society disapproves of the divorced and single adult and merely tolerates the widowed adult. Our society is structured around the couple and our normal social activities are designed for couples. The single adult disrupts the pattern. Thus, when remarriage occurs, an approved status is obtained and the persons involved are reinstated into the social fabric. For this reason, then, it was expected that the reconstituted family would find acceptance or, at worst, indifference. Two of the remarried wives expressed it this way:

People are surprised when they find out this is a combined family. There's no stigma. Everyone thinks it's wonderful that Lenny got married and that I got married. It's much better than being widowed and divorced.

I think both our families were happy about our marriage. His family is very affectionate and they just welcomed me with open arms. The divorce caused more talk and questions than the remarriage.

One of the husbands who found acceptance had the following to say:

Everyone likes everyone and everyone approves.

Our friends and families couldn't be happier about our marriage.

A doctor who married his nurse after he was divorced remarked:

One of the things we worried about was our patients. But we have notes and letters and everything. It turned out more beautiful than my highest hopes. Everyone is so happy for us. They're just tickled to death. We're thrilled. They treat us just as they used to.

Two of the couples who found indifference noted:

One in a while we get some very simple questions and we give very simple direct answers. Most people don't seem the slightest bit interested after a while.

I think the children were worried about attitudes toward them until they found out no one was going to raise eyebrows at them. They thought they would be in the limelight but people just ignored it.

One father who encountered a great deal of curiosity said:

There was lots of curiosity because of the double children situation. Neighbors mostly, not family. Stupid neighbors ask, How do the children get along? Do they listen to you? They want to know about my ex-wife. How often does she see the kids? Does it bug them that she doesn't come very often? Those are the main questions. Another one is when are we going to start having children of our own!

One husband told the investigator how he and his wife escaped from the disapproval:

In the beginning my family wasn't completely for

my getting married. I resented it. They identified with my previous wife. My wife and I moved away from where I used to live to avoid some of these problems.

Some of the most painful rejection comes from parents. One stepmother, married to a widower, said:

I've had lots of difficulty with the boy's grand-parents, which has led to tension in my marriage. My husband and I cannot come to any agreement in this area. I think if my husband's ex-in-laws were not in the picture, the situation would be easier to deal with and there would be less tension.

Other rejected remarried people noted:

My family is hard to get along with, especially my mother. She resented my remarriage because she raised my son for three years after my wife died and then I took him away.

My grandmother has always objected to my marriage to a woman with kids. I don't pay any attention to her though. She'll never get over it because she's from the old country and she thinks differently. She shows my wife her feelings. She always has.

My parents disapproved of my marriage. They thought I was too old. I was living with my parents and supporting them. [My marriage] upset them. It [was] a source of a lot of our arguments. It's changed now. They live in a senior citizens house and the tension has eased.

CHANGES IN THE PERCEIVED ATTITUDES OF OUTSIDERS

Table 7.4 shows the close similarity between the answers given by men and women. Apparently only a very small percentage believed attitudes toward themselves were worsening. Of those who felt attitudes had remained the same, twenty-seven of the men and twenty-eight of the women believed the attitudes had been good from the start. It appears, then, that most of the subjects' kin were perceived as having favorable attitudes toward the reconstituted families.

The same variables will be examined here as were examined earlier, with the addition of the type of marital dissolution and whether or not the couple were of the same religion.

TABLE 7.4

	Changes in Outsiders' Perceived Attitudes			
	Husband		Wife	
Direction of Change	percent	number	percent	number
Worse	2	(2)	6	(5)
Same	35	(30)	35	(30)
Better	23	(20)	19	(18)
Total	60	(52)*	60	(53)*

*Forty percent of both the men and the women could not indicate in which direction change had occurred in outsiders' attitudes. Percentages are based on the total N of 88.

Age

Fourteen percent of those under forty and ten percent of those over forty felt rejection. Thirty-two percent and 25 percent respectively felt indifference. Fifty-four percent of the younger people and 65 percent of the older felt their kin accepted them. It was anticipated that older people would be most accepted by the kin group. Given our societal norms, families and close friends would be concerned when a person over forty, especially a woman, was unmarried, because they would feel the person might be facing long years of loneliness and insecurity as he or she gets older and chances for remarriage diminish. Therefore, when the person does remarry, it would not be surprising that relatives would approve. The findings in this study indicate that age did not affect outsiders' attitudes, and most of the people believed they were getting approval, regardless of their age.

Length of previous marriage

Fifteen percent of those who had previously been married less than ten years and 8 percent of those who had been married over ten years felt rejected. Twenty-five percent and 27 percent of each group felt indifference. Sixty percent and 65 percent, respectively, felt accepted.

The data suggests that the length of the previous marriage is not a factor in the giving or withholding of kin approval for remarriage. Apparently families were pleased when relatives remarried regardless of how long they had been married before.

Religion

Protestants were divided as follows: 15 percent were in the "Rejected" category; 19 percent in the "Indifferent" category; and 66 percent in the "Accepted" category. This compares to 9 percent of the Catholics in the "Rejected" group; 42 percent in the "Indifferent" classification; and 49 percent who felt accepted.

There are too few Jews and unaffiliated people in the sample for consideration. Only Protestants and Catholics were compared, without regard to sex, because the differences between the men and the women were infinitesimal. There were no differences between the two groups in terms of rejection. Forty-two percent of the Catholics felt indifference from their family and friends compared to only 19 percent of the Protestants. Only 49 percent of the Catholics compared to 65 percent of the Protestants believed their kin approved of the reconstituted family.

Protestants, then, felt they were given more approval and less indifference when they became part of reconstituted families than Catholics. The difference can be accounted for in terms of the Catholic church's attitude toward divorce and remarriage. That is, it recognizes divorce and remarriage only between widowed people or widows and single people. The Catholic church espouses the view that marriage is regulated by divine and natural law; it still opposes divorce and remarriage after divorce. It was expected that the Catholics in this study would be disapproved of by their family and friends on the grounds that divorce and remarriage are sacrilegious.

In this sample of twenty-eight men who were Catholic, 50 percent had been divorced, 35 percent had been widowed, and 15 percent had never been married before. Of these, 46 percent were married to women who had been divorced, 14 percent to widows, and 40 percent to single women. Of the twenty-seven Catholic women, 44 percent had been divorced, 7 percent had been widowed, and 49 percent had never been married before. Sixty-three percent of these wives were now married to divorced men, 22 percent to widowers and 15 percent to men who had been single.

These figures seem to show that disapproval of divorce and of remarriage of divorced people accounts for the lack of approval the Catholics in this study experienced. One-half of the men had been divorced and almost one-half were married to divorced women. Forty-four percent of the women had been divorced and 63 percent were married to divorced men. Approximately one-half of both sexes, then, were either divorced themselves, married to divorced people, or both; and approximately one-half of these people felt approval from their family and friends.

Religious difference

TABLE 7.5

	Religious Difference and Perceived Outsiders' Attitudes							
Religious difference	OAS							
	Rejection		Indifference		Acceptance		Total	
	%	#	%	#	%	#	%	#
No difference	13	(9)	22	(15)	65	(43)	100	(67)
Difference	10	(2)	50	(10)	40	(8)	100	(20)
Total		(11)		(25)		(51)		(87)*

*One couple did not give their religion.
Note: G = .03

Table 7.5 reveals that kinship groups were more likely to accept reconstituted families and were less indifferent when there was no religious difference. August B. Hollingshead found that next to race, religion is the most decisive homogamous factor.[6] Leonard Benson believes that religion "is not as important today as it was at the time of his [Hollingshead's] study, but it still carries weight."[7] Benson also notes that studies on the religious factor in marriage are rare and only one state, Iowa, records such information on marriage license applications. However, it is known that interreligious marriages occur most often between very young couples and older couples and between remarrying couples.[8]

We might speculate that most parents and close friends and relatives prefer to see their family members marry someone of the same religious background and are likely to feel that an interfaith marriage would be "beyond their tolerance limits."[9] Although subjects were not asked about religion directly, this study seems to corroborate this speculation and to extend it beyond family attitudes toward first marriages and into the area of remarriage.

Social class

TABLE 7.6

Social Class and Perceived Outsiders' Attitudes							
Social class	OAS						
	Rejection		Indifference		Acceptance		Total	
	%	#	%	#	%	#	%	#
Working	12	(2)	35	(6)	53	(9)	100	(17)
Middle	12	(6)	38	(18)	50	(24)	100	(48)
Upper middle	13	(3)	5	(1)	82	(19)	100	(23)

It was anticipated that the upper middle class would be the least indifferent to and the most approving of the reconstituted family because of their greater concern with kin relationships than either the working or the middle class.

Table 7.6 bears out this expectation. There was no difference between the three social classes in terms of rejection by family and friends. There was also no difference between the working class and the middle class in terms of indifference, while the upper middle class showed considerably less indifference than the other two classes. It also offered more approval than either the working or the middle class. Compared to working-class and middle-class families, upper-middle-class families are known to be the group most concerned with family ties and lineages because of economic interests and rules of inheritance, although not to the degree to which upper-class families are concerned with such things. Almost all of the upper-middle-class subjects in this study married within their social class. Therefore, it is not surprising that the respondents from the upper-middle-class category were most approving when one of their members remarried and preserved the continuity of the family's life.

Previous marital status

Because it has roots deeply imbedded in the Judeo-Christian tradition, marital stability is morally approved of in our society. Therefore, divorce may be considered by many to be a sign of moral failure. In addition, our society is without ethical imperatives which would force relatives and friends to feel constrained to give support (both material and emotional) to divorced people. This is in contrast to the expected support at the time of widowhood. Therefore, it was anticipated that divorced people would receive the least acceptance of the three categories and the widowed the greatest acceptance.

TABLE 7.7

Previous Marital Status and Outsiders' Attitudes						
	OAS					
Previous marital status	Rejection		Indifference		Acceptance	
	%	#	%	#	%	#	Total
Divorced	14	(15)	26	(27)	60	(63)	(105)
Widowed	5	(2)	26	(10)	69	(26)	(38)
Never married	15	(5)	39	(13)	46	(15)	(33)

Table 7.7 reveals that there was no difference in kin attitudes toward divorced and widowed men and women in a remarriage. However, when the husband or wife had never been married before, there was considerably less acceptance. This is difficult to explain and there is little in the data to supply reasons. One man who had never been married before and who was in his twenties at the time of his marriage to a divorced woman with children remarked that his family felt he was too young to be "burdened" with the responsibility of another man's children. Another male respondent in his forties at the time of his first marriage mentioned that his elderly parents resented his moving out of their home

and giving them less of his time and income. One woman mentioned that her husband's family rejected her because her husband supported her children by her first husband.

Perhaps, then, those who had never married before did not receive approval to the degree that divorced and widowed people received it because their families and friends either felt they were being imposed upon in the reconstituted family or were jealous because attention had been diverted from themselves to the new spouse.

To summarize briefly this section on kinship attitudes toward reconstituted families, as perceived by the subjects, 13 percent felt rejected, 59 percent felt accepted, and 28 percent felt their families were indifferent. Almost all subjects believed the relationships had either remained unchanged or had improved over time. Neither the ages of the remarried people nor the length of their prior marriages influenced the outsiders' attitudes. Protestants, both men and women, found more acceptance and less indifference than Catholics. The same was true for intrafaith remarriages. Upper-middle-class people were more accepted than either working- or middle-class people. Those who had never been married before received the least amount of family approval.

OUTSIDERS' ATTITUDES
AS AN INDEPENDENT VARIABLE

It was noted before that families cannot live in a vacuum, and the attitudes of outsiders, which may include families of orientation, extended family members, and close friends, may well have an impact on the internal relationships of the reconstituted family. Therefore, the effects of the outsiders' attitudes on the relationships between the stepparents and the stepchildren (PCRS), on the husband-wife relationship (HWRS), on the relations between stepsiblings (SSRS), and on the family's integration (FIS) were examined.

Stepparent-stepchild relationship

Analysis of the data shows that among those who had been rejected by family and friends, 54 percent had a "Poor to good" PCRS and 46 percent had an "Excellent" PCRS. Among those whose kin groups were indifferent to them, 48 percent were in the "Poor to good" category and 52 percent were in the "Excellent" category. For those whose families approved of the reconstituted family, 27 percent were in the "Poor to good" category and 73 percent were in the "Excellent" category.

The stepparent-stepchild relationship, then, was not influenced if kin groups ignored or rejected the family. However, when the outsiders were accepting, the stepparents were more likely to attain "Excellent" relations with their stepchildren.

It is probable that when outsiders approve of a remarriage, they are helpful to their remarried relative. Parents may assume grandparental roles; sisters and brothers may take on the responsibilities of aunts and uncles. The result would probably be that the children and the stepparents feel they are part of the family, and both are, therefore, more comfortable in their new roles within the reconstituted nuclear family as well as in the extended family.

Husband-wife relationship

Of those subjects who felt rejected by their families, 54 percent had a "Poor to good" HWRS and 46 percent had "Excellent" scores. Of those whose relatives were indifferent, 72 percent had a "Poor to good" HWRS and 28 percent had "Excellent" husband-wife relations. Of those whose families were accepting, 31 percent had a "Poor to good" HWRS and 69 percent had "Excellent" scores on this variable.

The findings indicate, not surprisingly, that when outsiders were accepting of the new family, the HWRS was more likely to be high. However, the data also show that rejection had a more beneficial effect on the HWRS than indifference. It may be that when a couple felt that their relatives rejected them, they tended to become closer to each other in a "two against the world" stance. The number of cases, eleven, precludes making any definitive remarks about this possibility. The only findings that seem notable are that approval is better for the relationship between the husband and wife than either rejection or indifference, but rejection may be more desirable than indifference.

Stepsibling relationship

Of the forty-five families with two sets of stepchildren, five were rejected by outsiders, nine met indifference, and thirty-one were accepted. The number of cases makes it difficult to draw any conclusions beyond the fact that outsiders' approval seems to have some effect on the relations among stepsiblings in the same way that it affects the husband-wife relationship. Both rejection and acceptance were better for the stepsibling relationship than indifference.

Family integration

Forty-five percent of those who had been rejected had "Low" family integration and 45 percent had "High" family integration. It would seem, then, that when outsiders rejected a reconstituted family, the rejection caused one extreme or the other. Either the family felt the rejection and could not cement their relationship or the rejection had the opposite effect and tended to weld the family together. Indifference apparently did not affect family integration. Thirty-six percent of those whose families were indifferent were in the "Low" family integration category, 32 percent were in the "Moderate" category, and 32 percent were in the "High" category. Acceptance seems to be correlated with "Moderate" and "High" family integration, with 40 percent and 50 percent in those categories, respectively, and only 10 percent in the "Low" category. There was, then, a moderately strong relationship between outsiders' attitudes and family integration.

In summary, acceptance from kin group led to higher Stepparent-Stepchild Relationship Scores. Indifference seemed the most detrimental attitude in stepsibling relationship scores (SSRS). Outsiders' attitudes were not very important in the total family integration, although indifference was probably the least helpful attitude.

SUMMARY

Outsiders were divided into ex-spouses and families and friends. Of the 176 people in the study, 54 of the men and 51 of the women had living ex-mates. The data showed that, in general, men had more problems with former wives than women had with former husbands. This finding was attributed in part to the fact that men may be averse to paying alimony when they have new families. Visitation may be a source of irritation between divorced people with the visiting husband usually bearing the brunt of it, and jealousy on the part of the present wife may exacerbate negative feelings between former spouses.

It seems that most remarried people are largely indifferent toward their ex-spouses; although more men than women in this study had negative feelings. Young women felt more indifference and had less positive feelings than older women; for men, age was not important. Neither the length of a prior marriage nor membership in a religious group were factors. There was less indifference and more negative feeling among middle-class people than among either the working or upper middle classes.

Family and friends were considered to be in one category because of the norm in this country that those most loved, most often seen, and most often associated with are "relatives," whether or not they are so in any biological or legal sense. There was little difference between the men and the women in their perception of kin attitudes. A combined score revealed that 13 percent of the people felt rejected, 28 percent felt their relatives were indifferent, and 59 percent felt they were accepted. Twenty-three percent of the husbands and 19 percent of the wives believed there had been changes for the better over the years in the attitudes of their relatives.

Neither age nor length of previous marriage were factors associated with outsiders' attitudes for either men or women. Protestants were accorded more acceptance and less indifference than Catholics. Interfaith marriage resulted in less acceptance and more indifference. Upper-middle-class people, regardless of sex, were more likely to be accepted than people of the other two classes. Finally, both widowed and divorced people received more acceptance than those who had been single before the present marriage.

Acceptance from outsiders helped to promote better relations between stepparents and stepchildren and between husbands and wives. There was little influence on the relations among stepsiblings, although the paucity of cases precluded any real understanding. Finally, either acceptance or rejection seemed to help create better family integration than indifference.

8/Summary and conclusions

As the major findings of the study are summarized, it must be kept in mind that the reconstituted families described may not be representative of all reconstituted families in the United States. Furthermore, because this study was concerned with a narrow substantive area (the inter-relationships of the members of a reconstituted family and the influence on that family of certain important outsiders), the research was of an ex post facto nature. Although the merits of the controlled experiment are recognized, there is much to be said in favor of the exploratory approach. There are times when the social scientist must, out of necessity, and should, out of desire, de-emphasize the scientific method and permit his or her own impressions to guide the analyses of the data. The conclusions of this study, then, are based in part on the observations and perceptions of the investigator.

To a degree, however, this has been a scientific endeavor. As such, the validity of the assumptions, interpretations, and conclusions must be questioned. Certainly much of the evidence is scanty, partly because of a paucity of subjects and partly because of the crudity of the measures used. Despite the apparent consistency, it is not impossible that some of the relationships are spurious and some may be stronger than the findings reveal. Obviously, then, this study has opened several Pandora's boxes.

This study deals with three types of American families: the traditional family, the reconstituted family, and the ideal family. The traditional family is monogamous and permanent, and retains its numerical dominance among types of families in the United States. It is a nuclear family consisting of the breadwinner husband, the homemaker wife, and their children; the family lives apart from any other relatives.

The second type, the reconstituted family, is composed of a man and a woman, at least one of whom has been previously married and has a child or children from that prior marriage.

The ideal type family is imaginary; that is, it represents the way Americans like to think their families are. The fact is, of course, that such a family does not exist in reality, and many sociologists have commented, both seriously and in fun, on the ideal family.

Willard Waller, tongue in cheek, said, "According to Victorian ideology, all husbands and wives live together in perfect amity; all children love the parents to whom they are indebted for the gift of life; and if these things were not true, they should be, and even if one knew that these things were not true, he ought not to mention it."[1]

An unknown wit defined the family as "a group of people somewhat haphazardly assembled at least initially, related by blood or by marriage and ruled by its sickest member."[2]

Hadden and Borgatta defined the American ideal family satirically.[3] The male is expected to be somewhat older than the female, although both should be relatively young. Both should be mature, responsible, rational, sensible, able to adapt, and aware of their own and each other's motives and needs. In American society, choice of mate is free, based on love. Each member of the pair is expected to feel that this love is a new experience and that each was made for the other. Although the choice is supposed to be open, young people in this society are encouraged to select someone of the same or at least similar race, ethnic background, religion, and educational level.

Marriage is seen as an institution which has characteristics that cannot be found outside it. A couple should be companionable; there should be open and free communication, support, and security. A husband and wife ought to give to, rather than take from, each other. Marriage includes freedom of sexual expression, without taboos, sanctions, guilt, or repression, although the wife should be a virgin at the time of the marriage.

The best part of the marriage should be in having children together. The number of children and their spacing should be the mutual decision of the couple; two or three children are considered the proper number. Married couples ought to allow themselves a few years alone together before beginning these families, but it is good to have children while young. Children are considered essential for the completion and happiness of the family.

Hadden and Borgatta assure the reader that they could have continued this description of the ideal American family except that the violinist was getting tired of playing "Hearts and Flowers!"

· Waller, the unknown humorist, and Hadden and Borgatta have supplied us with some not-so-humorous descriptions of the ideal family.

Let's examine some classical definitions of the American family and then attempt a new definition. This is no simple task for several reasons. For one, American culture is pluralistic and has derived from many nations, which means there may be contradictory values involved. For another, the ideal family image has undergone rapid change during the last century, particularly during the last decade. The changes are primarily reflected in the attitudes of a small percentage of younger adults and have not yet significantly altered the traditional ideal American family image. No one knows, as yet, how long lasting or how widespread these changes will be. Bell and Vogel have said:

> We shall regard the family as a structural unit composed, as an ideal type, of a man and woman joined in a socially recognized union and their children. Normally, the children are the biological offspring of the spouses, but as in the case of adopted children in our society, they need not necessarily be biologically related. This social unit we shall call the *nuclear family* or simply the

family. This unit is familiar and easily identifiable in American society, and it is the expected household unit.[4]

Another sociologist stated that the term *family* generally refers to the nuclear family, which he defined as "the socially sanctioned cohabitation of a man and a woman who have preferential or even exclusive enjoyment of economic and sexual rights over one another and are committed to raising the children brought to life by the woman."[5]

There are, of course, other definitions of family. However, definitions will not necessarily describe the ideal type of family, which is our concern here. How can we utilize the definitions already mentioned, along with others, in formulating a description of the ideal type American family? It must be stressed that this ideal type is based on antiquated traditional values. Nevertheless, some 30 to 35 percent of the families in America come close to being ideal. Most important, it is the model which the majority of the subjects in this study were striving to emulate.

Structurally, the ideal American nuclear family contains an adult male and an adult female and two children, one of each sex. The adults are married and the biological parents of the children. Each member of the family is expected to behave in certain socially prescribed ways. There are three key statuses in the family: man, woman, and child. There are also three key role relationships within the family subsystem: husband-wife, parent-child, and sibling-sibling. Finally, there are two key roles external to the subsystem. One of these is the function of the adult male; that is, he is the connecting link between the family group and the world outside because his position in the occupational hierarchy determines the social class position of the family. The other, the function of all members, is the maintainance of relationships with kinship and friendship groups outside of the nuclear family.

The adult male's primary role is that of breadwinner. It is his task to provide sufficient income for the family's comfort and security. The wife's primary role is that of homemaker. It is her responsibility to care for the house, to prepare meals, to maintain a comfortable, inviting, clean atmosphere for family living. The primary role of children comes in later life, when the parents have grown old. As children, they are expected to be obedient and respectful and to perform well in the outside world so as to bring pride to the family unit. However, childrens' obligations have changed so radically over the past century that it is almost impossible to define them clearly.

If these three types of families were to be compared, the expectation would most likely be that the reconstituted family would come closest to the ideal type, because the reconstituted family holds the traditional family as a high value. More than any other type, the reconstituted family subscribes to the notion that the best type of family is the traditional, monogamous, permanent American family. One remarried woman stated it this way:

> Nothing pleases my husband as much as having strangers tell him my daughter looks like him. He gets embarrassed if anyone knows she is a stepdaughter. I guess we all like it better when people take us for a regular family.

This study has shown that certain variables—the husband-wife relationship, the stepparent-stepchild relationship, the stepsibling relationship, and outsiders' attitudes—had an effect on family integration, but to varying degrees. The degree to which the reconstituted family is the ideal family may be estimated. Bear in mind that the stereotyped division of labor, as set forth in the traditional nuclear family, may be totally or partially absent. In reconstituted families, tasks are not always rigidly defined as man's, woman's, or children's work.

THE HUSBAND-WIFE RELATIONSHIP

It was found that of the eighty-eight couples in the sample, 7 percent rated a "Poor," 39 percent rated a "Good," and 54 percent rated an "Excellent" HWRS. All the factors which could possibly affect this relationship could not, of course, be examined, but of the eight variables that were looked at, three seemed to have great influence. The first of these was the education of the husband. If the husband had attended college, his relations with his wife were directly affected in a positive manner. Educational level for women seemed to be unimportant in the marital relationship.

The second influencing variable was prior marital status. For both men and women, the husband-wife relationship was rated higher if death had been the means of terminating the previous marriage of at least one of the partners. Again, for both sexes, the relationship was most adversely affected if the prior status had been bachelorhood, implying that any marital experience, even if poor, is better than none at all in remarriage.

Social class was the third important variable affecting this relationship, with the quality of the relationship varying directly with social class position: the higher the social class, the better the relationship.

Age was not relevant to success in remarriage, nor was religious affiliation a factor. Interfaith marriage did not influence the relationship between the husband and wife. Finally, age, sex, and residence of the children from former marriages had no appreciable effect on marital relationships.

In general, the men and women in reconstituted families were anxious to be successful and happy in their new marital relations. Most of them had experienced what they believed to be failure in situations of divorce, or tragedy in situations of widowhood. Those who had not been married before somehow identified with their spouses in the past failure or tragedy.

According to Leonard Benson, in most societies there is "marriage work"[6]—the basic obligations that couples assume when they marry. Among these are 1) truthfulness and dependability, which means that husbands and wives are expected to be honest with one another and to be reliable; 2) sharing the work, which implies a division of labor which each is expected to recognize and fulfill; 3) ego support and sympathy, which demands that partners be sensitive, tolerant, and understanding toward each other; 4) talking and listening, which includes companionship, friendship, and confidentiality; 5) sexual satisfaction, which implies faithfulness and a desire to please; and 6) volunteering, which means that married couples are expected to give more to each other than just routine attention.

Using Benson's description of marriage work, how well

did the remarried couples fulfill the basic obligations? With few exceptions, the subjects felt that their new mates represented an improvement over the past. They seemed to "work" at making the marriage successful, expending a great deal of self-conscious effort to perform well and to make one another "happy." One husband said:

> I think you have to work at marriage. First there must be communication. We talk everything over together. Then there must be cooperation. You have to always do more than [what] you think is a fair share. If both people are doing more than they think is expected, you can't miss. Finally, I think you must give attention to each other—no matter how busy you are outside.

And another woman remarked:

> It's a lot of work to be married and you have to think about it, especially the second time. You have to give of yourself, of your time and your love. Marriage is a business.

One value these people stressed was communication. The remarried parents seemed to feel that they would be unable to avoid problems and that the best way to resolve them is to be direct and open with one's mate. One wife stated it this way:

> I think our marriage is a good one because we're able to communicate and to express our feelings. You must be patient and tolerant—but mostly, you must communicate.

Many of the remarried people had gone into this second relationship with misgivings, apprehension, and severe doubts. One man noted succintly at the close of the interview, "In this second marriage I expected the worst and found the best!"

Expectations concerning romance and passion were diminished. These people appeared to be more interested in comfort, in peaceful lives, and in companionship. Most of all, the remarrying parents hoped to find mates who would love their children and serve as surrogate parents. Several mentioned this expectation and only one man said that he felt the children were a secondary consideration. Probably because of this expectation the most severe problems centered around the children. One wife told the interviewer:

> Ours is an average marriage. I've had lots of difficulty with my stepson's grandparents, which has led to tension in my marriage. I consider some of our arguments serious to the point, at times, that I think the marriage may have been a mistake. The arguments are all about my stepson.

Sometimes the problem arises because the second wife is jealous of the time her husband gives to his nonresident children. One such husband noted:

> Our biggest problem is my children. I think there are times when my wife thinks I devote too much time to them. When you see them once a week you don't discipline them as if you lived with them; and there's a tendency to try to pack a lot of attention and love into a short time.

In summary, then, the remarried people in this study were quite satisfied with their situations. Most were more satisfied than they had anticipated. Most conveyed the impression that they believed their spouses were fulfilling the obligations noted above by Benson. Most believed the present marriage was happier than the first had been.

It seems fair to state, then, that a review of the data indicates that the remarried husbands and wives performed all of the marital tasks quite well. Perhaps remarried people are more appreciative of their situations than people married only once. They have experienced the loneliness and ambiguity of the single adult in American society. They have learned to modify expectations so they more closely resemble reality. Most of them are grateful to become half of a "couple" again. One woman summed it up:

> Remarriage is very wise, [and] so much better than remaining alone. In many ways it's more difficult

than the first time you marry, especially if you have children in the picture; but on the other hand, it can be easier because you are older and wiser and have learned from past experience.

THE STEPPARENT-STEPCHILD RELATIONSHIP

It was found that of the eighty-eight families in the sample, 18 percent had "Poor to good" stepparent-stepchild relationships, and 64 percent had "Excellent" relationships.

Protestant stepparents were more likely to achieve a good relationship with their stepchildren than any other religious group, although the finding is more significant for stepfathers than it is for stepmothers. The age of the stepfather was not an influence in his relationship with his stepchildren. Younger stepmothers were more likely to have good relationships with their new children than older stepmothers. When the stepmother had been widowed, she was more apt to develop a good relationship with her stepchildren than a divorced or previously unmarried stepmother. However, stepfathers who had never been married before formed better relationships with their stepchildren than stepfathers in either of the two other categories. Social class was found to be directly associated with stepparent-stepchild relationships, although the association was a weak one.

The age of the stepchild was not important in the relationship with the stepfather, but stepmothers were able to develop better relationships with their stepchildren when the children were under thirteen years of age. Furthermore, women seemed to get along better with their stepchildren if their own children lived with them. And when a remarried couple had children together, both parents achieved a higher PCRS with their stepchildren than when no children were born into the new marriage.

The husband-wife relationship was associated with the parent-child relationship. When the husband and wife did not have a good relationship, the stepchild and stepparent usually failed to achieve a good relationship. The inference can be made, then, that the relationship between husband and wife influences the relationship between the stepparent and the stepchild.

Of all the dyadic relationships in reconstituted families, the one between stepparent and stepchild seemed to be the most worrisome to the stepparent. This may have been partly because of the undefined roles and obligations. There is a negative mythology surrounding the stepparent-stepchild relationship, producing negative expectations, which are not easily, and never entirely, surmounted. Furthermore, for most people the relationship is a new one. Almost all of the subjects had experienced marriage and parenthood before, but none had ever been a stepparent. Because, then, of the mythology, the negative expectations, and the lack of experience and normative guides, this relationship was approached by our subjects with a certain amount of trepidation.

There are also great differences between being a stepmother and being a stepfather, although both roles are more difficult than being a parent. For one thing, the stepmother suffers from a terrible reputation, set forth in such tales as Cinderella. The role can be made more complicated if the child sees the stepmother as having taken the father from the real mother. All the resentment felt toward the father may be projected onto the stepmother. The stepfather has fewer problems, if for no other reason than he is usually away from the house for longer periods of time. Nevertheless, there is frequently some resentment directed toward the stepfather if only because the child has lost some attention he or she had before the mother remarried.

Relationships with stepchildren, finally, seemed to turn on two things. One is frequency of interaction. The more people are with each other, the more they come to like each other. Thus, if the stepchild and the stepparent lived together, the chances were greater that they would become attached to one another.

Second is the attitude of the stepchild. Many of the adults felt they wanted to be close to the children, but for one reason or another, the children held them off. Two stepmothers expressed it this way:

> If I had a friend who was marrying a man with children I'd advise her to try to give them a lot of love, but [not to] expect that love to be returned as if [she] were a real parent.

> The thing [you have] to learn is not to push your-

self on the children. Don't go overboard or be overanxious. Just go along and play it cool. Let them come to you. Accept whatever kind of relationship they want to establish. Be a friend or a mother, whatever they want from you. Don't say, "I want to be a mother to you."

Just as there is "marriage work," there is "parent work."[7] In the past the most difficult part of parent work was physical, but today, with physical tasks simplified by mechanical devices, the stress is on the psychological side of parent work. The six tasks of parent work are: 1) maintenance, which means the parents must provide for the survival of their children by seeing to it that they have food, shelter, clothing, and physical care; 2) guidance or socialization, which means that parents must provide moral teaching and transmit the values, beliefs, and goals of the society; 3) discipline, which parents must apply in order to teach self-restraint and compliance with behavioral norms and standards; 4) assistance in growing up and in coping with life situations (assistance may take the form of advice, instruction, and/or financial help); 5) love and respect, which are regarded as an obligation of parents to children (they are not to be treated as objects to be manipulated nor as inferior beings to be exploited, but as people with feelings and rights); and 6) release, or letting the children go when the time is right for them to leave the family home (parents are expected to train their children to be independent and to help them separate themselves from the nuclear family when they are mature enough to do so).

With Benson's description as a guide, the performance of the stepparents was evaluated. Actually, of course, the stepparent role is not the same as the parent role, although some stepparents tried to assume it. One problem in this society is that there is no defined stepparent role, so that a person in that status is frequently confused as to his or her duties and obligations. The situation is further complicated by the residence of the stepchildren. A stepmother whose stepchild has been half-orphaned and lives with her has a very different relationship with that child than one whose stepchild has both parents living, lives a thousand miles away with the biological mother, and comes to visit for the summer. Between these two extremes are many other confounding factors, such as the attitude of the biological mother, the financial situation, the relationship between the remarried father and the child, and so on. Nevertheless, Benson's were the only criteria on which to base an evaluation of how well the reconstituted family performed its parental functions.

The first function mentioned was maintenance, meaning that it is the responsibility of parents to provide food, clothing, shelter, and physical care for their children. This task was well discharged by the stepparents. Although money was frequently considered a problem because of alimony payments and/or child support payments, very few of the stepparents resented the need to spend money on stepchildren, especially if the children were residents of the household. One mother commented:

> He doesn't mind paying for my children. Our money situation is a little tight now, but he never complains.

Even when the relationship between the stepfather and the stepchildren was a poor one, there seemed to be little resistance to spending money on the stepchildren. One father said:

> My marriage isn't too good. I think it may improve when the kids get out, not until. The kids are the big thing. We have no trouble about money. I pay for just about everything. The father gives a little support, I don't know how much it is. This isn't what bothers me. I don't mind paying, but the whole thing hinges on her kids. It will make a vast difference when the kids are out of the house. There will always be resentment between us.

The second function of the family is socialization. Parents are expected to provide guidance in moral issues and to transmit the values, attitudes, and beliefs of the society to the children. It appears that in this area the stepparents did not play a big role. If the child did not live with the step-parents, there was little or no socialization. Even when they shared the same residence, the stepparent was likely to defer to the real parent. One father expressed it in the following fashion:

> I don't think my stepsons treat me like a real father. They don't come to me for advice or help in anything. I think they hesitate because I'm not their real father, even though I feel responsibility for them. I think I hesitate myself to take on the complete role of father.

Another father, whose children lived with his former wife, said:

> My kids are very reserved in their affections for my wife because they adhere to the old standards that [their real mother taught them]. Is this out of loyalty? I think they realize that my wife would have been a better mother had they been lucky enough to have her, but now they stick to their mother's way of doing things.

The family also is supposed to discipline children, teach self-restraint. This seemed to be a problem area in recon-stituted families. Fathers of visiting children preferred not to discipline them because they wanted to use the visitation time for recreation, love, and strengthening the relation-ship. One wife remarked:

> I feel I don't get a chance to enjoy my step-children because my husband is too easy on them. He says you can't do that [punish] to your kids when you don't live with them. I think he should—that's his job as a father. This way they run wild and it's no picnic for me.

On the other hand, many fathers who lived with their wife's children felt the wife was too lenient and didn't discipline her own children sufficiently. However, most of these stepfathers did not feel they had the right to discipline the children, even though they believed the children needed it. One husband said:

> She is always making it up to her kids because she divorced their father. I think she feels guilt for their sake. Anyway, there's nothing I can do about it. I like them and all, but they aren't my kids. Besides I think my wife's kids resent me. I don't know why. They're not real fond of their father and I've never really tried to take the place of their father. I think none of us really knows where I stand with them.

When it comes to giving advice or instruction, it seemed that many of the stepparents and the parents of "visiting" children held back in this area as well as in the area of discipline. One stepmother of a pre-teen-age girl commented:

> I really would like to fuss with her more. You know, help her pick clothes and fix her hair. But I guess I'd better not get mixed up in her mother's territory. She likes me now and will take some advice if I'm careful. I don't want to spoil anything by making waves.

Another stepmother who had in the past attempted to be motherly finally gave up. She said:

> What has worked for me in the last two times my stepdaughter has been here is to try not to change her at all. I don't say, Go take a bath, or It's time for bed, or Don't talk with food in your mouth. I put a wall around me. I just let her alone although she is here. And she and I get along much better. She told her dad on the way to the airport that she had the best time she ever had. I actually worked at doing that. Of course it wouldn't work if she lived in the house. No one realized I was doing it.

Benson puts giving love and respect together as one obligation of a family toward children. However, the stepparents in this study were very careful to separate the two items. Most felt they did receive respect from their stepchildren; but only a handful felt they were loved. However, this appears to have been the stepparental expectation and the stepparents seemed to be satisfied to get respect, even if they were not loved. One stepmother told the interviewer:

> I get along fine with my stepdaughter. She's respectful and obedient and she takes discipline when necessary. I'm very satisfied. She doesn't treat me like a parent and I can't say she loves me, but we never have any disagreements on anything.

Another stepmother believed the situation would change over time:

> I love my stepson very much. I'd love to get custody [of him]. Usually the first few hours or days that he's here, he's kind of strange. We both know there is a lot of talk in his home against me when he is here. But we figure that when he gets older he will know that I'm not the bogeyman his mother's trying to make me out to be. Otherwise, we get along very good.

There were very few stepparents who reported wholehearted love for their stepchildren. Many expressed varying degrees of affection and others were optimistic about change in the future; but strong feelings of love were rarely expressed. One father, an example of this small segment of the sample, said:

> I feel very strongly toward my stepdaughter. I love her very much. I have adopted her to bring her closer to the family. I love her as much as I do my own kids. She's ours, since we're married. It's like, to me, she's never had a father. Her attitude toward me also is very good. We play together. She accepted me as her father a long time ago.

It is not possible to report on the capability of stepparents in terms of the last function Benson suggests—release, when the children are ready to leave home. None of the children in this study were over eighteen and therefore the question did not arise.

It should be clear that it is difficult to completely separate these functions from each other. Most of the stepparents tried very hard; most of the parents were supportive of these efforts. Too often, however, the absent biological parent had a detrimental effect on the stepparent-stepchild relationship, because he or she would influence the children against the stepparent, especially against the "evil stepmother." Sometimes there are uncontrollable factors involved. A widowed stepmother, now married to a widower, said:

> My daughter wanted a father and she has really been happy. She was old enough so that she appreciated what it is to have a father around. They're very close. He's very proud of her. He boasts about her all the time. It's very different [with] me and my stepson. Tom's mother had only been dead a year when we were married. I have an entirely different relationship with Tom. We get along very well; I've never had any problems, but I cannot say that our relationship is truly a mother-son relationship in a lot of ways. I guess the difference between him and my daughter is that he remembers his mother, whereas my daughter doesn't remember a father because he died when she was eighteen months old. My daughter has no possibility of comparison. I know I can't expect too much more with Tom than we have."

Of the six tasks performed by parents, the stepparents rated high when faced with maintenance of the children and stepchildren. They also appeared to earn the respect of the stepchildren. However, feelings of love did not seem to obtain either from the stepchildren to the stepparent or vice versa, although the stepparents seemed to have made a greater effort to build loving relationships than the stepchildren. Finally, most stepparents left discipline, advice, and socialization in the hands of the stepchild's biological parent.

THE STEPSIBLING RELATIONSHIP

Only forty-five families in our sample contained at least one child from each parent, so that a stepsibling relationship was present. Of these, 24 percent were found to have generally "Poor" stepsibling relations, and 38 percent had "Good" and "Excellent" stepsibling relations.

Various factors helped to account for the differences in these relationships. One is the residence of the children. A somewhat higher percentage of stepsiblings were rated "Excellent" if they lived in the same house with each other. A second finding was even more meaningful. If the remarried parents had a child or children together, the relationship between their children from prior marriages was greatly enhanced.

The mother's education was not a factor in the relationship between her own children and her stepchildren. On the other hand, fathers who had not attended college were more likely to have children and stepchildren who got along well together. Similarly, the mother's age was of no importance, but fathers who were under forty were more apt to have children and stepchildren who liked each other.

Two other variables seemed to be important in these relationships among stepsiblings. If the parents had a successful marital relationship and if the stepparents had good relations with their stepchildren, then the stepsiblings were more likely to have good relationships with each other.

Finally, social class and stepsibling relationships varied inversely. Working-class children had the highest scores, middle-class children had the next highest scores, and upper-middle-class children had the lowest scores.

According to Donald P. Irish,[8] sibling work includes 1) socialization, in which older children teach younger ones how to interact interpersonally and how to respect the rights of others;[9] 2) serving as substitute parents, when parents are otherwise engaged; 3) teaching skills, both social and manual; 4) providing emotional security; 5) providing companionship; 6) providing challenge and stimulation;[10] and 7) in its resemblance to the husband-wife dyad, the older brother-younger sister relationship can be seen as socialization for marriage.[11]

There were several remarks made by the adults in this

study which showed how important it was to be seen by outsiders as a "normal" family. Comments from two stepfathers illustrate this:

> The kids act like real brothers. They gang up on my wife. They fight and argue all the time, like real brothers. They share and really accept one another.

> The kids all intermingle and fight and act like all brothers and sisters. It's not "Mine against yours." They stick together.

The second most typical comment indicated how the children also seemed to share this need to be seen as "real" brothers and sisters. For example, one parent stated:

> The kids get along fairly well together. There's no real hatred and at the same time, no real love, I don't think. But when they are in public, they always refer to each other as brother and sister.

The emotion mentioned most often was jealousy, but with their need to be seen as "typical" American families, most of the parents believed, or said they believed, that this emotion was to be found in any family. One husband remarked:

> They really act like brothers and sisters. They all steal from one another; they tattle on each other. There is some jealousy, but like [that of] normal siblings. My wife's older child may be really jealous because she was once the oldest child. They don't act as if they are two groups. My four kids are a pretty tightly knit group. They got that way about six months before the divorce.

Several parents felt that the greatest deterrent to their children and stepchildren being close was a large age difference. Most mentioned this with a touch of wistfulness, as if things would have been much better if the children had been closer in age. One mother said:

They are not like brothers and sisters. There's no real intimate relationship because of the age difference. It's the real siblings who stick together and do things for each other. The stepsiblings [are] like polite strangers. Maybe the age difference helped because it kept them too far apart for hostility to grow.

A father mentioned:

The kids are very concerned about each other. They don't see each other too much but they constantly ask about each other and how they are doing. It's unfortunate that age and geographical locations keep them from seeing each other. I think if they did see each other frequently they would be very close.

There were those parents and stepparents who blamed themselves because the children did not get along with each other. One father told the interviewer:

The kids get along pretty well together. There was some tension at the beginning because I was paying more attention to my daughter and everything was new. But now they refer to each other as brother and sister. There doesn't seem to be any rivalry. They share things and they all stick together. They are closer now that they know each other better and I don't show so much partiality.

Several parents indicated that they could not account for the lack of warmth between their children and stepchildren. One husband said:

The two sets of kids just don't get along. I really don't know why. They may have resented my getting married, although I didn't really discuss it with them. The kids weren't really close to their mother, so that doesn't explain anything. I guess to some extent they resent my marriage. I don't

know why. We tried a little, sort of, to bring the
two sets of kids together. They are just altogether
different personalities, that's all.

From the comments of most of the respondents who had
two sets of children in the family, it appears that only a few of
the children performed the expected "sibling work." The
remarks below are from parents whose children were doing
this "work":

The children get along well. They like each other
very much. Each worries about the other. It isn't
the usual thing because they have played together
since they were two and three. I've known his former wife about twelve years. They are like brother
and sister and refer to each other that way.

I have never once heard them fight. I wish my
daughter would get along as well with her sister all
the time. My stepson and daughter get along
fabulously. There is some rivalry for their father's
attention, but like any siblings. When he goes
home, my daughter sobs.

The two girls are like sisters. The older boys pro-
tect each other.

The division in our family is between the older
kids and the younger ones. The two older ones
have now gotten to the point where they even
have the same friends. The older boy keeps coming home from school because he is so happy to
have a home and all the brothers and sisters
around. There is some jealousy between the two
younger girls, but not because they are stepsisters; [their fights are] just like real sisters' fights.
The older two treat the younger two just like any
kids [would]—as if they are pests.

In sum, then, the roles that can be performed by siblings
for each other did seem to be performed in reconstituted
families by the stepsiblings, although not often. Most of the

functions were being performed by the parents for the children, were not being performed at all, or the real siblings were enacting the roles for each other. Nevertheless, with few exceptions, the stepsibling relationships were tolerable. Occasionally, they were extremely bad and the children either avoided seeing each other if they could or the situation in the home came close to being unbearable.

On the other hand, there were some stepsibs who got along very well and who seemed to have grown close and loving, protective and helpful, supplying friendship, companionship, security, and challenge. This was rare. The most important finding was that all members of the reconstituted family needed to be seen as a "normal" family. This need, variously stated, was expressed over and over again: "They fight and compete like any real siblings;" "They love each other and help each other, like any real siblings;" "They don't get along too well, but in public they act like brother and sister." The reconstituted family, then, needs to be seen as "typical."

OUTSIDERS' ATTITUDES
AND THE RECONSTITUTED FAMILY

Relationship with former spouse

Fifty-four husbands had living ex-spouses. Of these, 41 percent said the relationship was a negative one; 43 percent said it was indifferent; and 16 percent said it was positive. Fifty-one wives had living ex-mates. Twenty-nine percent of the relations were negative; 59 percent were indifferent; and 12 percent were positive. Although the wives were more likely to feel indifferent toward former spouses and less likely to feel negative than husbands, the majority of people—51 percent—felt indifference, compared to 35 percent who felt negatively and 14 percent who felt positively.

Four variables—age, length of previous marriage, religion, and social class—were tested to ascertain their influence on the relationship with the former spouses. Age was not found to be a factor for the husbands, but younger wives were more apt to feel indifferent and less apt to have positive feelings than older wives. Husbands and wives who had previously been married less than ten years were less indifferent and more positive in their feelings toward ex-spouses than those previously married ten years and over.

Religion was not a factor for men, but Protestant wives appeared to be less indifferent and more positive than Catholic wives.

Both husbands and wives in the working class were more likely to be indifferent toward former mates than people of higher classes, and none of the working-class wives had positive feelings toward their former husbands.

The ex-wife seemed to affect the reconstituted family in two ways. She directly influenced the children by causing visitation difficulties and adverse feelings toward their other parent and toward his spouse. Indirectly, she may cause the second wife to be jealous of whatever attachment, real or imagined, her husband may still have for her.

Finally, the second wife may be angry when money goes to the ex-wife. Several parents had a great deal to say about ex-wives:

> His girls might be jealous of me because their previous mother told them I was just a stepmother. The younger stepgirl hasn't been too respectful to me lately. She goes to see her mother about once a month. We have problems when she comes back. She's afraid of her mother. She loves me but she's afraid to let me know for fear I'll leave. Her mother is at the root of the whole thing. She can't stand to see how happy the children are with us. She remarried about six weeks after the divorce. She didn't want to see the children then, but she does now, just to split us up.

> I don't see my children often enough. My ex-wife didn't make it very easy. It was my right to visit them every Sunday and she was not supposed to ask any questions, but as it was, I felt very intimidated by her. I don't know why. Even after the divorce, I felt obligated somehow to keep quiet and play along. I could never go out and get mad. The situation now is that I don't have [my] children any more.

> When we were first married I resented his ex-wife to a certain extent because of my inability to have children with him. After that I only resented the

money they got. When my husband's first wife left her husband she never quite broke off the relations with her neighbors here and for this reason I had a very tough time. She was very close to the neighbors and it is a very sensitive thing with them. I don't fit in with the neighbors.

I see my daughter about once a year. I don't see her too much so I don't create any animosities with the mother. There isn't any resentment on my former wife's part; there was just a lot of hardships with the divorce and I don't want to stir anything up.

My daughter hardly ever comes to see me. She doesn't seem to want to talk and she is not friendly to either my wife or myself. I think she only comes out of duty. There is a great deal of tension around her visits. I think she has deep feelings for me, but I would guess that exposure to her mother has spoiled her feelings.

The ex-husband affected the reconstituted family less and in a different sense. Usually he was resented more by his former wife than by her husband. The resentment most often centered on money: the wife felt her ex-husband should send more money or send it more regularly:

My husband has adopted my children and they don't see their real father very much. My ex-husband agreed to sign the adoption papers, mostly because then he wouldn't have to support them. But there isn't any tension about it. At first when he used to see them more often and made very irregular payments, there was tension, but now that Johnny has adopted them, the visits are fine and very infrequent. I sometimes wonder if there isn't a little tension on the children's part.

If the present husband harbored angry feelings toward his wife's ex-spouse, they centered on the children more than on money. He was likely to feel that the former husband should be more attentive to his children. When the

119

stepfather said he was fond of the children, the researcher tended to feel that his remark about the real father's attention was not quite honest, but, rather, that the stepfather was happy that the responsibility of the children now rested with him. There was some indication that resentment on the part of the stepfather was socially expected:

> I think [the situation with my wife's ex-husband] is not very good and I'm a little disappointed in their father because he doesn't care enough for [the children]. He takes them here and there for occasions, but I don't think [he does enough]. As far as his coming here, I don't like the situation when he comes. He usually comes to get them and takes them some place else. I don't think it's as it should be. It's hit-and-run. He doesn't seem to have enough time, in my estimation, for his own boys. He comes less and less over the years. He doesn't make the big fuss as much as he used to. He's like a flash in the pan. I think if [they] were my boys, I'd be different. He doesn't support them. There's a court order, but nobody's enforced it. We don't care one way or the other.

> My wife's ex-husband doesn't visit here at all. I think that nothing could come from his visits because of the type of individual he is. So I would prefer that he wouldn't [come]. However, I would not disagree too much if he wanted to come. If the children or Marie felt that it was important, then I would agree. I would wish he would not come. I'm sure Michael wishes he would come. He has a definite need for his dad. The two older children seem not to need the father and so I doubt very much whether they even think about [him] at all. I don't think they care.

Both ex-husbands and ex-wives, then, exerted some influence on the reconstituted family. Usually this influence was negative. Ex-wives caused difficulty by influencing the children's attitudes toward their fathers and their fathers' present wives. They frequently caused jealousy on the part of the new wife. Ex-husbands aroused feelings of resentment because they either did not support the children or the payments were not regular. Furthermore, they became targets for the present husband's moral indignation by neglecting, in the stepfather's opinion, the children.

Family and friends' attitudes

Men and women were almost in complete agreement in terms of the attitudes of their kin toward their reconstituted family. Thirteen percent felt rejected, 28 percent felt the kin were indifferent, and 59 percent felt accepted.

The same social factors that had been tested for the relationship with ex-spouses were examined in order to see the effects of the attitudes of kin. Two more variables were added: previous marital status and religious difference.

Again, the age of the male was not important, while young women were more likely to feel accepted. Length of former marriage was not a factor for men, but women who had been married for longer than ten years were more apt to feel acceptance. Both Protestant husbands and wives were more likely to feel accepted than Catholics; Catholics were more likely to believe their kin to be indifferent. Acceptance was greater and indifference less when there was no difference of religion. Working- and middle-class people felt almost exactly the same about their kin groups' attitudes; but the upper-middle-class people experienced a great deal more acceptance and less indifference. Men who had been widowed believed their families to be most accepting and those who had been single believed them to be least accepting. There was no difference in acceptance between divorced and widowed women, but women who had never been married before found the least amount of acceptance from kin groups.

A direct association between outsiders' attitudes and parent-child relationships was found. Those who were accepted by outsiders also had "Excellent" relations with their stepchildren. The same equivalence held for the husband-wife relationship. Those who felt themselves accepted had the best relationship with their present spouse. There seemed to be no association between outsiders' attitudes and the relationship of stepsiblings.

The remarried couples in this study spoke overwhelmingly of curiosity. Almost all of them mentioned that at the beginning of the marriage there had been many questions from family members, friends, neighbors, and even their children's teachers. Below are some of the most commonly asked questions.

Does it work?

Why does the boy live here and not with his mother?

How much do you pay in child support?

How's the marriage going?

How do the children get along?

Do the children listen to you?

How often does your ex-wife see the children?

Does it bug you that your ex-wife doesn't come more often?

When are you going to have children of your own?

What about her first husband?

Do the children pit you against one another?

How come the children don't look alike?

Most of the subjects told the interviewer that they answered the questions if they weren't too personal. Several remarked that they were not embarrassed or ashamed of the situation, but the majority seemed to prefer that people view them as having a traditional family rather than a reconstituted one. Others said they were very annoyed at being questioned and refused to reply. One husband tried to explain the reason for the enormous curiosity:

> I find all kinds of reactions. Some people are curious because they would like to know what would happen to them if they had the same thing happen. I don't think they question the children; they question me. They want to know all the details.

Another reaction the subjects spoke of was an attitude of initial disapproval, or at least withholding of approval, which changed over time.

> I think when we first got married certain of my so-called friends were maybe a little bit belligerent, which was surprising because it was not [my] friends that I thought would be that way. My first wife's relatives are closer to my present wife right

now than they are to me. They have accepted her.

The only outsiders who have had an effect would be relatives. It's lessened now that we've been married two and a half years. Nobody expected us to get married and nobody expected us to stay married. There were lots of little picky things like talking behind backs. On his side it was based on the fact that I had been married and had a child; on my mother's side it was based on the fact that she was worried he would not take care of [my child].

In our own families there had been some curiosity and sometimes they tried to cause a little trouble. There used to be questions quite a lot. I told them to mind their own business. I don't care about the past; it's over and done. What he did before is none of my business. It's what we do now that counts.

Finally, there were a great many subjects who had the wholehearted support, approval, and encouragement of their kindred from the beginning.

Our families, friends, and neighbors were very encouraging. They all thought we should have gotten married sooner.

Everyone was pleased about our marriage. Her mother especially. Even her other husband's mother was glad.

My mother was a widow for many years and she was very happy when I married. She didn't want me to go through that.

Our families, even my first mother-in-law, like my wife, Patty, tremendously. We see her [first mother-in-law] often.

Reconstituted families, then, usually believe that their kin-group members are curious about their lives and the lives of their children and stepchildren. Most of them parried questions, although several were willing to answer freely. Rejection seemed to be taken rather philosophically by our subjects; but when there was acceptance, it was welcome and appreciated. Those who faced indifference claimed that they felt indifference in return and tried not to let it affect their new families. The answers to the questions concerning outsiders' attitudes clearly reflected the subjects' preoccupation and anxiety about being considered a traditional family. This was the outstanding reaction to the attitudes, whether negative, indifferent, or positive, that the subjects felt were expressed by outsiders. What counted was that they should not appear "different" from whatever they believed was the "typical" American family.

These, then, are the major findings in this study. Obviously, much has been left unexplored and much has been left unexplained. Therefore it is important to point out certain areas for future work:

1. How self-conscious are the efforts reconstituted families make in order to present themselves as traditional families? How are the efforts manifested? Who among the members makes the greatest and who the least effort?

2. How different are the relationships between stepsibs when they live together and when they don't? Since most of the half-siblings in this study were less than two years old, what kind of relationships are likely to obtain between older half-sibs?

3. What are the relationships and attitudes within lower-class families? Upper-class families? Black families?

4. What are the effects on the reconstituted family of such variables as "length of previous marriage" and "prior type of marital status?" (With so few people in the "widowed" and "never married before" categories, our findings are far too inconclusive.)

These are, of course, only a few of the many possible research problems arising from this study. Others, more peripheral, might include an investigation and comparison of the lives of people raised as stepchildren and of people from primary families. One might examine reconstituted families which contain parents married more than twice, wherein there may be three or four sets of stepchildren rather than only one or two. More work must certainly be done to uncover the reconstituted family's position within the cultural system. How does it influence the society and how does the society influence it? All these and many more are provocative questions for future research.

COMPARISON OF IDEAL, TRADITIONAL, AND RECONSTITUTED FAMILIES

This study takes as one of its basic assumptions that the reconstituted family strongly values an image of itself as the ideal-type American family. It is self-conscious about its status as a reconstituted family and it makes great efforts to appear to be, and in fact to be, as "typical" as possible. In order to test this assumption, a comparison was made between the reconstituted and the traditional families to see which came closest to the ideal-type family.

Below is a chart which shows the major characteristics of the ideal-type American family in column one. Column two shows what research has revealed about the traditional family. Column three shows what this study discovered about the reconstituted family.

TABLE 8.1

Ideal-Type Family, Traditional Family, and Reconstituted Family Compared		
Ideal Type	Traditional	Reconstituted
Unit contains one adult female and one adult male, somewhat older.	Unit contains one adult female and one adult male, approximately 2.3 years older.[12]	Unit contains one adult female and one adult male, approxi-six months older.
Unit contains two to to four children.[13]	Unit contains average of 2.7 children.[14]	Unit contains average of 4.0 children.
Children are biological offspring of male and female.	Children are biological offspring of male and female.	Forty-two percent (37 families) had natural children, with an average of 1.3 in each family.
Husband and wife are	Mean age of men at	Mean age of men at

TABLE 8.1 — Continued

Ideal Type	Traditional	Reconstituted
in early twenties at time of marriage.	time of first marriage is 22.8; mean age of women is 20.5.[15]	time of remarriage is 35.0; mean age of women is 34.6.
Husband and wife of same religion.	Rate of interfaith marriage for all major religions is 6.4.[16]	Twenty-three percent (20) contained husbands and wives of different religions.
The husbands and wives are members of the same race.	Only 1.2 percent of all marriages are interracial.[17]	Non-Caucasians were not included in this study.
Husbands and wives belong to same ethnic group.	This varies by ethnic group, with Italians having the highest percentage of endogamy (82%) and Scandinavians the lowest (18%). The average endogamy rate for all groups is 64%.[18]	Endogamy rates were not ascertained in this study.
Husbands and wives are in the same social class.	The overwhelming tendency in the United States is toward homogamy.[19]	Thirty-six of the wives in this study were employed, with 12 percent in the professorial/managerial class, compared to 27 percent of the men in the same category. The discrepancies were even greater in the blue- and white-collar categories.
The husband-wife relationship is the strongest tie in the nuclear family, affecting all other relationships.	Loss of love is the primary "real" grounds for divorce. Family integration is threatened when marital relationship is unsatisfactory.[20]	This relationship had an effect on all other relationships in varying degrees. Of those with excellent HWRS, 67 percent had a high FIS; 73 percent had a high PCRS score; 32 percent had a high SSRS; and 69 percent felt acceptance from kin.
The selection of a mate is a matter of free choice.	Americans have free choice within surprising legal, cultural, and parental limitations.[21]	The subjects in this study had a free choice of mate from a field of eligibles which was narrow compared to primary mate choices because of age and parenthood.

TABLE 8.1 — Continued

Ideal Type	Traditional	Reconstituted
Husbands and wives are mature, responsible, rational, dependable, and supportive.	Married people have no more or less of these qualities than unmarried people in the population.	These qualities, per se, were not measured in this study; but it can be assumed that remarried people would not differ in such areas from married and unmarried people.
Husbands and wives are companionable, understanding, honest, and trustworthy.	Companionship is considered the most valued part of American marriage, particularly in sharing leisure time activities.[22]	Ninety percent of the subjects in this study felt they were companionable with their spouses. Eighty-six percent of the wives and eighty-nine percent of the husbands felt they and their spouses were trustworthy and honest.
Husbands and wives love each other.	Seventy-eight percent of white, urban wives felt satisfied with their love relationships with their spouses.[23]	Ninety percent of the wives and 93 percent of the husbands felt loving toward and loved by their spouses.
Husbands and wives have good sexual relationships.	There is no research to indicate sexual satisfaction in marriage; but there are indications that a high percentage of marital sex is unsatisfactory. Some of these indicators are psychological and some include the suspected high incidence of wife swapping.[24]	Fifty-two percent of both men and women in this study believed their sexual relationships were excellent.
The husband's primary role is that of breadwinner.	Research shows that this is a changing area of family life.[25] Nevertheless, "the division of labor in the modern family coincides with the division of labor in the traditional family."[26]	One hundred percent of the husbands in this study were the major breadwinners in the family.
The wife's primary role is that of homemaker.		Forty-one percent of the wives in the study had occupations; yet they considered their work role secondary to their role as homemaker.

TABLE 8.1 — Continued

Ideal Type	Traditional	Reconstituted
Having children is a vital aspect of marital satisfaction.	Only 3 percent of the wives in the Blood and Wolfe study said they never have and never would want to have children. Having children was associated with high marital satisfaction.[27]	Forty-two percent of the couples in the samples had children together. Of these 37 couples, 54 percent rated their husband-wife relationship as excellent, 40 percent rated it good, and 6 percent rated it poor.
Children live with their parents.	There is no research available, but it is reasonable to assume that close to 100 percent of the minor children in the United States live with their parents, the exceptions being in the lowest social strata and in the upper strata where children are often in boarding schools.	Fifty-four percent of the fathers and 89 percent of the mothers had their children from former marriages living with them.
Parents are responsible for the financial maintenance of their children.	While there is no research on this topic, it is reasonable to assume that most parents, except in the lowest strata, assume financial responsibility for their children.	Of the sixty-six fathers who had children under twenty-one, 56 percent said they paid all their children's expenses and 42 percent said they paid only part of their expenses. Of the fifty-nine men who had stepchildren under twenty-one, 69 percent paid all their stepchildren's expenses, 19 percent part of them, and 12 percent paid none.
Parents are the primary socializing agents of the children, including giving advice and administering discipline.	"In today's American middle class, parents are less involved in the socialization of their children than they were in the past.	Fifty-three percent of the sixty-six stepfathers and 25 percent of the seventy-two stepmothers said they had parental feelings towards their stepchildren and acted in the socializing agent role.
There is mutual love between parents and	Specific information is unobtainable, but	Of the sixty-six stepfathers, 45 per-

TABLE 8.1 — Continued

Ideal Type	Traditional	Reconstituted
children.	it is logical to assume that in early childhood there is a great deal of mutual love; in adolescence children question their love for their parents;[29] and there is a return of loving feelings as children mature.	cent said their stepchildren felt loving toward them and vice versa. Of the seventy-two stepmothers, 18 percent felt that there was mutual love between themselves and their stepchildren.
There is mutual respect between parents and children.	Specific information is unobtainable, but it is logical to assume the same conditions prevail in this area as they do in the area of mutual love.	Forty-seven percent of the sixty-six stepfathers, and 41 percent of the seventy-two stepmothers claimed there was mutual respect between themselves and their stepchildren.
There is "togetherness" in the American family. That is, parents and children share many values and enjoy being and doing things together.	There is a loose, yet definite, youth subculture which has special values, special music and dress, and a special language, quite separate from the adult culture and not well understood by adults.[30]	Forty-two percent of the sixty-six stepfathers, and 32 percent of the seventy-two stepmothers reported that they spend a great deal of time with their stepchildren.
Older chidren act as surrogate parents by serving as stimulators, protectors, and socializers.	"Thus far, social scientists have rarely attempted to conduct statistical studies to explore the significance that brothers and sisters have for each other."[31]	Of the forty-five families containing two sets of stepchildren, 38 percent had poor relations, 38 percent had good relations, and 24 percent had excellent relations.
The nuclear family maintains good relationships with kin and friendship groups.	"The nuclear family must be viewed within the context of a structure of kin-related units which provide services and aid in an exchange system based on reciprocity, opportunity, and choice."[32] The "neolocal nuclear family is . . . closely integrated	Fifty-nine percent of the families in this study believed their families and close friends accepted their reconstituted families.

TABLE 8.1 — Continued

Ideal Type	Traditional	Reconstituted
	within a network of mutual assistance and activity which can be described as an inter-dependent kin family system."[33]	

There are twenty-four items in the characterization of the ideal-type American family, which was compared to the traditional family and to the reconstituted family. The traditional family was very similar to the ideal type in thirteen of these items, partially similar in four items, different in three items, and there was no available data for four items. The reconstituted family was very similar to the ideal type in four items, partially similar in sixteen items, different in one item, and data had not been collected for three items.

Since the degree of similarity is difficult to ascertain, we can say that the traditional family is at least partially similar to the ideal type in seventeen of the twenty-four characteristics and the reconstituted family is at least partially similar in twenty of the characteristics. Thus, the assumption that the reconstituted family tries to approximate the ideal type seems upheld. There are indications that in time the reconstituted family will become even more like the ideal type. There are two reasons for this assumption.

First, as noted above, most of the characteristics of the reconstituted family are only partially similar (not very similar) to those of the ideal type family. There is, however, evidence to support the notion that in several of these characteristics the reconstituted family will come to be very similar to the ideal type.

TABLE 8.2

	Worse		Same		Better		
Relationships	percent	number	percent	number	percent	number	Total
Husband-wife	6	(10)	24	(39)	70	(108)	(157)
Parent-child	7	(10)	45	(66)	48	(70)	(146)
Stepsibling	16	(7)	42	(38)	42	(38)	(83)
Outsiders' attitudes	6	(7)	57	(60)	37	(38)	(105)

Changes in Relationships

Table 8.2 indicates that these families were still in a state of flux. A large number of the relationships were changing. To illustrate, in the husband-wife relationship which is, as in the ideal type and in the traditional family, the key relationship, 76 percent of all subjects reported change. Of these, 70 percent felt the relationship was improving. By "improving," these subjects meant they were becoming more like the ideal type. The research families, therefore, cannot be regarded as "finished," and only time will show how similar to the ideal type they become as the relationships become less elastic, and as this type of family becomes more institutionalized.

The second reason for assuming that the reconstituted family may become more like the ideal type is the self-consciousness of the reconstituted family. Self-consciousness is the crux of the difference between the traditional and the reconstituted families. Couples were very much aware of what was going on in their reconstituted families, and most of them have tried and were still trying to be "natural" parents, to have "natural" families, in the ways they imagined such families to be. As one wife put it, "You must want to make it work. You have to keep on trying every minute."

These self-conscious attempts can best be illustrated by the remarks made by the subjects themselves. The following are examples of the sort of thing that almost every family member, especially those that were most successful, had to say. One mother, who had several children of her own and several stepchildren, in discussing the relationships among the children, remarked:

> I think our problem is trying to sort out what is "normal" sibling from what is "step." They may say something that is normal sibling, but we turn and we jump on them because we're sensitized. We keep telling them we're one family. We're going to be raised as one family. We have to learn to get along together. It doesn't always work, but that's what we tell them.

The mother of two children had this to say about her husband's relationship with her children:

131

They had a very big adjustment to make [among] the three of them. It was very bad at first, to the point where I didn't think it would work. It's improved 75 percent and the other 25 percent is like any parents. Some real parents have it worse. . . . [Remarriage] does work, it's possible, but you have to be very patient; you need lots of compassion because you're meshing lives that at one time didn't exist for each other. You can't fuse these lives overnight. It takes several years. Only the last year has been pleasant.

One thoughtful stepmother, who had been trying all through her marriage to form a good relationship with her stepdaughter, had this to say:

I suppose some of the problems that I face are the same as most parents with their own children. It sometimes is a comfort to me to talk with another parent and I realize it isn't just as a stepmother that I have these [problems]. I don't think my problems with Linda are basically too different from any mother and daughter.

The following remarks were made by a stepfather who had not been previously married. At the time of the interview he had one stepson and one daughter of his own in the present marriage.

I consider my relationship with my stepson quite often. I always question, Am I doing the right thing? Am I treating one child differently from the other? When you haven't been the father from the beginning, it's hard, but I'm trying. I'm still too unsure of myself in this role, but I've tried very hard to be what I consider a father image. It took getting used to; but I'm used to it now and I feel better about it.

One man summarized the feelings of many of the subjects in this study when he commented:

You have to make a conscious effort, realize there
are some problems, and work them out so you can
become a real family.

In conclusion, then, the majority of the reconstituted
families seemed to be making self-conscious and sincere
efforts to form families that are as similar as possible to what
they considered "natural" families (what really amounts to
the ideal-type American family). These families appeared to
be aware of the problems involved and most felt that, with
constant work and attention, they would succeed in their
difficult and complicated task. The chances of the reconstituted family becoming like the ideal type are great
because the reconstituted families considered the ideal type
a value they were striving to attain.

Appendix A

SECTION A.   HUSBAND AND WIFE

QUESTION	HUSBAND	WIFE
How old were you on your last birthday?	1. _____	9. _____
What is your religious preference?	2. _____	10. _____
How far did you go in school?	3. _____	11. _____
What is your occupation?	4. _____	12. _____
	_____	_____
	_____	_____
How was your previous marriage terminated?	5. _____	13. _____
How many years were you married to your former spouse?	6. _____	14. _____

| How many of your own children from a former marriage live with you and what are their ages? | 7. _____ | 15. _____ |

| If they do not live with you, how often do they visit? | 8. _____ | 16. _____ |

17. SELECT THE NUMBER WHICH COMES CLOSEST TO THE FAMILY'S TOTAL YEARLY INCOME, INCLUDE EARNED INCOME FROM BOTH, CHILD SUPPORT, INVESTMENT INCOME, AND HELP FROM OTHERS.

1) Less than $5,000 _____
2) $5,000 to $9,999 _____
3) $10,000 to $14,999 _____
4) $15,000 to $19,999 _____
5) $20,000 to $29,999 _____
6) Over $30,000 _____

SECTION B & C.   WIFE AND HUSBAND INTERVIEWED SEPARATELY

DISCUSS THE FOLLOWING TOPICS. ANSWERS RECORDED ON TAPE.

18. *Visitation*

26.

19. *Relationship with Husband (Wife)*

27.

20. *Stepparent-Stepchild Relationships*

28.

21. *Relationships Among Step- and Half-Siblings*

29.

22. *Effects of Outsiders*

30.

23. *Stepfamily as a Total Group*

31.

24. SUGGESTIONS ON ANYTHING LEFT UNDISCUSSED.
32.
25. FINAL QUESTION: If you had a good friend who was thinking about forming a stepfamily, what advice would you give?
33.

SECTION D & E.   WIFE AND HUSBAND, SEPARATELY

Please answer the following question if both you and your spouse have children from former marriages. If not, just skip to the next question.

34. How do children from different marriages get along together?
42.

You will see two lines on the left hand side of the page. Fill in the name of one of your children in the first column, matched with one of his stepbrothers or stepsisters in the second column. Eventually, all possible pairs will be included. On the longer line to the right, place an X between "Very close" and "Very distant" to indicate how this pair of children feel about each other. Do this for each pair of children. If there are not enough spaces, please add some at the end.

Here is an illustration:

Wilma	Henry	/	X	/
Your child	Husband's child	Very close		Very distant
_____	_____	/ _____		/
_____	_____	/ _____		/
_____	_____	/ _____		/
_____	_____	/ _____		/

Please answer the following questions only if you have stepchildren.

35. I would like you to do the same thing you did in the previous question for yourself and each stepchild.

43.

Write the name of the child on the short line to the left and then place an X on the line between "Very close" and "Very distant" to indicate how you feel about this child. Draw more lines if needed.

For example:

Henry	/ _____ X _____ /
Husband's child	Very close Very distant
_____	/ _____ /
_____	/ _____ /
_____	/ _____ /

Please answer the following question only if your husband has stepchildren.

36. Please do the same as you did in the question above for your husband and his stepchildren.

44.

Write the name of your child on the short line to the left and place an X on the line between "Very close" and "Very distant" to indicate how you think your husband feels about your child. Draw more lines if necessary.

Here is an example:

Wilma	/ _____ X _____ /
Your child	Very close Very distant
_____	/ _____ /
_____	/ _____ /
_____	/ _____ /

37. Please indicate in the same way how happy you consider your marriage.

/‾‾‾‾‾‾‾‾‾‾‾‾‾‾‾‾‾‾‾‾‾‾‾‾‾‾‾‾‾‾‾‾‾‾/

Very happy   Very unhappy

45.

38. Please indicate in the same way how close you would say your whole family is as a group.

/‾‾‾‾‾‾‾‾‾‾‾‾‾‾‾‾‾‾‾‾‾‾‾‾‾‾‾‾‾‾‾‾‾‾/

Very happy   Very unhappy

46.

39. Which of the following things do you and your husband pay for, or plan to pay for in the future, or have paid for in the past for your children from a former marriage, if you have any; and for his children from a former marriage, if he has any?

Please check the appropriate space if you plan to pay for "all," "part," or "none." If the item has nothing to do with your family, please check the space under "not appropriate."

	Your children				Husband's children			
	All	Part	None	Not appro.	All	Part	None	Not appro.
Education	___	___	___	___	___	___	___	___
Dental expense	___	___	___	___	___	___	___	___
Camp	___	___	___	___	___	___	___	___
Medical expense	___	___	___	___	___	___	___	___
Vacations	___	___	___	___	___	___	___	___
Allowances	___	___	___	___	___	___	___	___

40. How often would you say you and your husband agree on the following things? Please circle the number which comes closest to your situation.

48.

Always	1
Frequently	2
Occasionally	3
Seldom	4
Never	5

a)	Money	1	2	3	4	5
b)	Recreation	1	2	3	4	5
c)	Bringing up children	1	2	3	4	5
d)	Religion	1	2	3	4	5
e)	Friends	1	2	3	4	5
f)	Each other's families	1	2	3	4	5
g)	Sex relations	1	2	3	4	5
h)	Politics	1	2	3	4	5

Now do the same thing—circle the correct answer—for the following questions.

Always	1
Frequently	2
Occasionally	3
Seldom	4
Never	5

i) Do you and your husband spend your leisure time together?
1 2 3 4 5

j) Are you candid with your husband? 1 2 3 4 5

k) Is your husband candid with you? 1 2 3 4 5

l) Do you and your husband like the same kinds of people?
1 2 3 4 5

m) Do you and your husband have serious arguments?
1 2 3 4 5

n) Do you show affection for your husband?
1 2 3 4 5

o) Does your husband show affection toward you?
1 2 3 4 5

41. In general, how do you think the following people regard your family? Please mark X on the line, as you did for past questions, to indicate how accepting or rejecting these people seem to be toward your family.

	Very accepting	Very rejecting
a) Your parents	/ _____	_____ /

b) Your brothers & sisters   /_____/
c) Your old friends   /_____/
d) Husband's parents   /_____/
e) Husband's brothers & sisters /_____/
f) Husband's old friends   /_____/
g) Your children's teachers   /_____/
h) Stepchildren's teachers   /_____/
i) Your children's friends   /_____/
j) Stepchildren's friends   /_____/
k) Neighbors   /_____/
l) Mutual friends   /_____/

Appendix B

This Appendix contains the tables which showed no or insignificant differences. Krushal Q was used to measure the amount of association for two-by-two tables; Goodman and Krushal's gamma was used for tables larger than two-by-two. Significance levels appear in a note below each table.

AGES OF REMARRIED HUSBANDS AND WIVES AT
THE TIME OF THE REMARRIAGE AND
FAMILY INTEGRATION

Age	Family Integration						Total
	Low		Medium		High		
	%	#	%	#	%	#	
Under 40	19	(17)	28	(25)	53	(48)	90
40 & over	24	(21)	40	(35)	36	(30)	86
Total							176

Note: G = .26

PREVIOUS MARITAL STATUS AND
FAMILY INTEGRATION

Previous marital status	Family Integration						Total	
	Low		Medium		High			
	%	#	%	#	%	#		
Divorce	23	(24)	43	(45)	34	(35)	(104)	
Death	15	(6)	18	(7)	67	(26)	(39)	
Never married before	25	(8)	25	(8)	50	(16)	(32)	
Total							(175*)	

*One wife did not reveal the manner in which her last marriage had been terminated.

Note: G = .24

LENGTH OF PREVIOUS MARRIAGE
AND FAMILY INTEGRATION

Length of previous marriage	Family Integration							
	Low		Medium		High		Total	
	%	#	%	#	%	#	%	#
Husband								
10 yrs. or less	23	(5)	45	(15)	40	(13)	100	(33)
Over 10 yrs.	26	(11)	31	(13)	43	(18)	100	(42) 75*
Wife								
10 yrs. or less	18	(7)	27	(11)	55	(22)	100	(40)
Over 10 yrs.	23	(6)	50	(13)	27	(7)	100	(26) 66*

*Thirteen of the husbands and 20 of the wives had never been married before. Two of the wives who had been married before refused to state how long the previous marriage had lasted.

Note: Q_{men} = .47
Q_{women} = .04

EDUCATIONAL LEVEL OF REMARRIED COUPLE
AND FAMILY INTEGRATION

Education	Family Integration						Total
	Low		Medium		High		
	%	#	%	#	%	#	
No college	29	(25)	29	(25)	42	(37)	87
College	16	(13)	38	(34)	47	(41)	88
Total		38		59		78	175*

*One husband did not reply to the question.

Note: G = .16

CHILDREN FROM PRESENT MARRIAGE
AND FAMILY INTEGRATION

Children from present marriage	Family Integration							
	Low		Medium		High		Total	
	%	#	%	#	%	#	%	#
No children	26	(13)	37	(19)	37	(19)	100	(51)
Children	16	(6)	30	(11)	54	(20)	100	(37)

Note: G = .28

SOCIAL CLASS AND FAMILY INTEGRATION

Social class	FIS							
	Low		Moderate		High		Total	
	%	#	%	#	%	#	%	#
Working	30	(5)	18	(3)	52	(9)	100	(17)
Middle	25	(12)	36	(17)	39	(19)	100	(48)
Upper middle	9	(2)	43	(10)	48	(11)	100	(23)
Total		19		30		39		88

Note: G = .01

EDUCATIONAL LEVEL AND HWRS

Education	HWRS					
	Poor to good		Excellent		Total	
	percent	number	percent	number	percent	number
Husband						
No college	60	(20)	40	(13)	100	(33)
College	35	(19)	65	(35)	100	(54)
Total		39		48		87*
Wife						
No college	46	(25)	54	(29)	100	(54)
College	44	(15)	56	(19)	100	(34)
Total		40		48		88

*Educational level for one husband was not ascertained.

Note: Q_{men} = .10
Q_{women} = .37

SOCIAL CLASS AND HWRS

Social class	HWRS					
	Poor to good		Excellent		Total	
	percent	number	percent	number	percent	number
Working	59	(10)	41	(7)	100	(17)
Middle	46	(22)	54	(26)	100	(48)
Upper middle	35	(8)	65	(15)	100	(23)

Note: G = .27

AGES OF STEPPARENTS AND PCRS

Age	PCRS					
	Poor to good		Excellent		Total	
	percent	number	percent	number	percent	number
Stepfathers						
Less than 40	33	(11)	66	(22)	100	(33)
40 & over	39	(21)	61	(34)	100	(55)
Stepmothers						
Less than 40	30	(17)	70	(40)	100	(57)
40 & over	48	(15)	52	(16)	100	(31)

Note: Q_{men} = .10
Q_{women} = .37

STEPPARENTS' RELIGION AND PCRS

Religion	PCRS				
	Poor to good		Excellent		Total
	percent	number	percent	number	
Protestant	28	(25)	72	(64)	89
Catholic	45	(25)	55	(30)	55
Jewish	40	(6)	60	(9)	15
Unaffiliated	53	(8)	47	(7)	15
Total		64		110	174*

*One couple refused to give their religion.
Note: G = .3

PRIOR MARITAL STATUS AND PCRS

Stepmothers	PCRS					
	Poor to good		Excellent		Total	
	percent	number	percent	number	percent	number
Divorce	37	(19)	63	(32)	100	(51)
Death	24	(4)	76	(13)	100	(17)
Never married before	45	(9)	55	(11)	100	(20)

Note: G = .03

SOCIAL CLASS AND PCRS

Social class	PCRS					
	Poor to good		Excellent		Total	
	percent	number	percent	number	percent	number
Working	41	(7)	59	(10)	100	(17)
Middle	38	(18)	62	(30)	100	(48)
Upper middle	30	(7)	70	(16)	100	(23)

Note: G = .14

RESIDENCE OF NATURAL CHILDREN AND PCRS

Children's residence	PCRS					
	Poor to good		Excellent		Total*	
	percent	number	percent	number	percent	number
Husbands						
At home	33	(13)	67	(26)	100	(39)
Away	39	(13)	61	(20)	100	(33)
Wives						
At home	33	(19)	67	(40)	100	(59)
Away	56	(4)	44	(3)	100	(7)

*Sixteen of the fathers and 22 of the mothers did not have children from former marriages.

Note: Q_{men} = .05
Q_{women} = .47

STEPCHILDRENS' AGES & PCRS

Ages of stepchildren	PCRS					
	Poor to good		Excellent		Total*	
	percent	number	percent	number	percent	number
Stepfathers						
Under 13	32	(10)	68	(21)	100	(31)
13 & Over	33	(12)	67	(23)	100	(35)

Note: Q = .01

AGE AND SEX OF WIFE'S STEPCHILDREN AND PCRS

Sex of step-child	PCRS									
	Under 13				13 & over				Total	
	Poor-good		Excell.		Poor-good		Excell.			
	%	#	%	#	%	#	%	#	%	#
Boy	24	(4)	76	(13)	50	(7)	50	(7)	100	(31)
Girl	26	(6)	74	(17)	50	(9)	50	(9)	100	(41)

Note: G = .01

CHILDREN FROM PRESENT MARRIAGE AND SSRS

Children from present marriage	SSRS							
	Poor		Good		Excellent		Total	
	%	#	%	#	%	#	%	#
Yes	34	(3)	22	(2)	44	(4)	100	(9)
No	39	(14)	42	(15)	19	(7)	100	(36)

Note: G = .28

RESIDENCE OF CHILDREN AND SSRS

Both sets of children home	SSRS							
	Poor		Good		Excellent		Total	
	%	#	%	#	%	#	%	#
Yes	33	(8)	38	(9)	29	(7)	100	(24)
No	43	(9)	38	(8)	19	(4)	100	(21)

Note: G = .2

PARENTAL EDUCATION AND SSRS

Education	SSRS							
	Poor		Good		Excellent		Total	
	%	#	%	#	%	#	%	#
Husband								
College	36	(9)	48	(12)	16	(4)	100	(25)
No college	40	(8)	25	(5)	35	(7)	100	(20)
Wife								
College	38	(5)	38	(5)	24	(3)	100	(13)
No college	38	(12)	38	(12)	24	(8)	100	(32)

Note: G = .2

PARENTS' AGES AND SSRS

Parents' ages	SSRS							
	Poor		Good		Excellent		Total	
	%	#	%	#	%	#	%	#
Husbands								
Under 40	20	(2)	20	(2)	60	(6)	100	(10)
40 +	43	(15)	43	(15)	14	(5)	100	(35)
Wives								
Under 40	27	(6)	45	(10)	27	(6)	100	(22)
40 +	48	(11)	30	(7)	22	(5)	100	(23)

Note: G = .8
    G = .14

HWRS AND SSRS

HWRS	SSRS							
	Poor		Good		Excellent		Total	
	%	#	%	#	%	#	%	#
Poor	100	(4)	0	(0)	0	(0)	100	(4)
Good	45	(7)	37	(6)	18	(3)	100	(16)
Excellent	24	(6)	44	(11)	32	(8)	100	(25)

PCRS AND SSRS

PCRS	SSRS							
	Poor		Good		Excellent		Total	
	%	#	%	#	%	#	%	#
Poor	88	(7)	12	(1)	0	(0)	100	(8)
Good	67	(6)	22	(2)	11	(1)	100	(9)
Excellent	15	(4)	50	(14)	36	(10)	100	(28)

SOCIAL CLASS AND SSRS

Social class	SSRS							
	Poor		Good		Excellent		Total	
	%	#	%	#	%	#	%	#
Working	38	(3)	25	(2)	38	(3)	100	(8)
Middle	44	(10)	30	(7)	26	(6)	100	(23)
Upper middle	29	(4)	57	(8)	14	(2)	100	(14)

Note: G = .1

SSRS AND FIS

SSRS	Family Integration							
	Low		Moderate		High		Total	
	%	#	%	#	%	#	%	#
Poor	66	(6)	33	(3)	0	(0)	100	(9)
Good	50	(9)	39	(7)	11	(2)	100	(18)
Excellent	11	(2)	39	(7)	50	(9)	100	(18)

EX-SPOUSES' ATTITUDES AND AGES
OF HUSBANDS AND WIVES

Ages*	Ex-Spouses' Attitudes							
	Negative		Indifferent		Positive		Total	
	%	#	%	#	%	#	%	#
Under 40	32	(18)	58	(32)	10	(5)	100	(55)
40 & over	38	(19)	42	(21)	20	(10)	100	(50)

*The ages were placed in two categories because of the paucity of cases.
Note: G = .05

LENGTH OF PREVIOUS MARRIAGE AND
EX-SPOUSES' ATTITUDES

Length of previous marriage*	Ex-Spouses' Attitudes							
	Negative		Indifferent		Positive		Total	
	%	#	%	#	%	#	%	#
10 yrs. or less	34	(22)	50	(32)	16	(10)	100	(64)
Over 10 yrs.	38	(16)	50	(21)	12	(5)	100	(42)

*The variable "length of previous marriage" was dichotomized because there were too few cases.
Note: G = .05

RELIGION AND EX-SPOUSES' ATTITUDES

Religion	Ex-Spouses' Attitudes							
	Negative		Indifferent		Positive		Total	
	%	#	%	#	%	#	%	#
Husband								
Protestant	36	(19)	45	(24)	19	(10)	100	(53)
Catholic	39	(11)	54	(15)	17	(2)	100	(28)
Jewish	22	(2)	67	(6)	11	(1)	100	(9)
Unaffiliated	33	(5)	54	(8)	13	(2)	100	(15)

Note: G = .03

SOCIAL CLASS AND EX-SPOUSES' ATTITUDES

Social class	Ex-Spouses' Attitude							
	Negative		Indifferent		Position		Total	
	%	#	%	#	%	#	%	#
Working	28	(5)	67	(12)	15	(1)	100	(18)
Middle	41	(24)	43	(25)	16	(9)	100	(58)
Upper middle	27	(8)	56	(16)	17	(5)	100	(29)

AGES OF HUSBAND AND WIFE AND OAS

| Age | OAS | | | | | | | |
| | Rejecting | | Indifferent | | Accepting | | Total | |
	%	#	%	#	%	#	%	#
Husband								
Under 40	12	(4)	33	(11)	55	(18)	100	(33)
40 & over	13	(7)	25	(14)	62	(34)	100	(55)
Wife								
Under 40	16	(9)	31	(18)	53	(30)	100	(57)
40 & over	6	(2)	23	(7)	71	(22)	100	(31)

LENGTH OF PREVIOUS MARRIAGE AND OAS

| Length of previous marriage | OAS | | | | | | | |
| | Rejecting | | Indifferent | | Accepting | | Total | |
	%	#	%	#	%	#	%	#
Husband								
10 or less	9	(3)	27	(9)	64	(21)	100	(33)
Over 10	12	(5)	29	(12)	59	(25)	100	(42)
Wife								
10 or less	19	(8)	24	(10)	57	(24)	100	(42)
Over 10	4	(1)	23	(6)	73	(19)	100	(26)

RELIGION AND OAS

| Religion | OAS | | | | | | | |
| | Rejecting | | Indifferent | | Accepting | | Total | |
	%	#	%	#	%	#	%	#
Protestant	16	(14)	19	(17)	65	(58)	100	(89)
Catholic	10	(5)	41	(23)	49	(27)	100	(55)
Jewish	7	(1)	33	(5)	60	(9)	100	(15)
Unaffiliated	13	(2)	33	(5)	54	(8)	100	(15)
Total		(22)		(40)		(102)		(175)*

*One couple would not give religious preference.

Note: G = .02

PREVIOUS MARITAL STATUS AND OAS

Previous marital status	OAS							
	Rejecting		Indifferent		Accepting		Total	
	%	#	%	#	%	#	%	#
Husband								
Divorced	15	(8)	28	(15)	57	(31)	100	(54)
Widowed	0	(0)	29	(6)	71	(15)	100	(21)
Never married	23	(3)	30	(4)	47	(6)	100	(13)
Divorced	14	(7)	23	(12)	63	(32)	100	(51)
Widowed	12	(2)	24	(4)	64	(11)	100	(17)
Never married	10	(2)	45	(9)	45	(9)	100	(20)

OAS AND HWRS

OAS	HWRS							
	Poor		Good		Excellent		Total	
	%	#	%	#	%	#	%	#
Rejecting	18	(2)	36	(4)	46	(5)	100	(11)
Indifferent	8	(2)	64	(16)	28	(7)	100	(25)
Accepting	4	(2)	27	(14)	69	(36)	100	(52)

Note: r = .296
r² = .08

SSRS AND OAS

OAS	SSRS					
	Poor to good		Excellent		Total	
	Percent	Number	Percent	Number	Percent	Number
Rejecting	80	(4)	20	(1)	100	(5)
Indifferent	100	(9)	0	(0)	100	(9)
Accepting	68	(21)	32	(10)	100	(31)
Total		(34)		(11)	100	(45)*

*Only 45 of the 88 families contained two sets of children from previous marriages.

Note: r = .097
r² = .008

OAS AND PCRS

OAS	PCRS							
	Poor		Good		Excellent		Total	
	%	#	%	#	%	#	%	#
Rejecting	36	(4)	18	(2)	46	(5)	100	(11)
Indifferent	32	(8)	16	(4)	52	(13)	100	(25)
Accepting	8	(4)	19	(10)	73	(38)	100	(52)

Note: r = .296
   r² = .08

OAS AND FIS

OAS	FIS							
	Low		Moderate		High		Total	
	%	#	%	#	%	#	%	#
Rejecting	45	(5)	10	(1)	45	(5)	100	(11)
Indifferent	36	(9)	32	(8)	32	(8)	100	(25)
Accepting	10	(5)	40	(21)	50	(26)	100	(52)

Note: r = .24
   r² = .06

RELIGIOUS DIFFERENCE AND HWRS

Religious difference	HWRS					
	Poor to Good		Excellent		Total	
	percent	number	percent	number	percent	number
No Diifference	41	(28)	59	(39)	100	(67)
Difference	60	(12)	40	(8)	100	(20)
Total		(40)		(47)		(87)*

* Religious preference was not ascertained for one couple.
Note: Q = .05

PRIOR MARITAL STATUS AND HWRS

Prior Status	HWRS					
	Poor to Good		Excellent		Total	
	percent	number	percent	number	percent	number
Divorce	49	(51)	51	(54)	100	(105)
Death	29	(11)	71	(27)	100	(38)
Never married before	54	(18)	46	(15)	100	(33)
Total		(80)		(96)		(176)

Note: G = .05

Notes

Chapter One

[1]These include: Alice Ruhler, "Das Stiefkind" in *Achwerezichbare Kinder,* Dresden, 1927; Fritz Wittels, *Die Befrenfung des Kindes,* Hippokrates Verlag, 4th ed., 1927; Erich Stern, "Beitrag zur Psychologie des Stiefkindes," *Zeitschrift für Kinderforeschung, 24* (1928), 144–57; and C. Hoenig, "Die Stiefeiternfamilie des Stiefkinders," *Zeitschrift für Kinderforeschung, 24* (1928), 188–331.

[2]Hannah Kuhn, "Psychologische Untersuchungen Uber das Stiefmutter-problem: Die Konfliktmoglichkeiten in der Stiefmutter-familie and ihre Bedeutung für die Verwahrlosung des Stiefkinds," *Zeitschrift für angewandte Psychologie, 45* (1929–1930), 1–185.

[3]R. Mudroch, "Das Stiefkind," *Versammlung für Kinderforeschung, 4* (Bratislava, 1932), 216–28; G. Neuman, "Untersuchungen uber das Verhaltnis Zwischen Stiefmutter und Steifkind," *Zeitschrift für Padagogosiche Psychologie, 34* (1933), 348–471; Warner Von Lincke, "Das Stiefmuttermotiv in Merchen der germanischen Volker," *Germanische Studien, 142* (1933).

⁴M. Fortes, "Step-parenthood and Juvenile Delinquency," *Sociological Review, 25* (1933), 153–58.

⁵Adele Stuart Meriam, *The Stepfather in the Family* (Chicago: University of Chicago Press, 1940); and "Stepfather in the Family," *Social Service Review, 14* (Dec. 1940), 655–77; Annie M. White, "Factors Making for Difficulty in the Stepparent Relationship with Children," *Smith College Studies in Social Work, 14* (1943), 242, Abs.; Janet Pfleger, "The 'Wicked Stepmother' in a Child Guidance Clinic," *Smith College Studies in Social Work, 17* (1946–47), 125–6, Abs.

⁶Else P. Heilpern, "Psychological Problems of Stepchildren," *Psychological Review, 30* (1943), 163–76; and Helene Deutsch, *The Psychology of Women* (New York: Grune & Stratton, 1944, 2 vols.). See especially Vol. 2, Chap. 12, "Stepmothers," 434–55.

⁷William C. Smith, *The Stepchild* (Chicago: Univ. of Chicago Press, 1953). Smith has also written several articles on the subject, including "The Stepchild," *Am. Soc. Rev., 10* (1945), 237–42; "Remarriage and the Stepchild," in Morris Fishbein and Ernest W. Burgess (eds.), *Successful Marriage* (New York: Doubleday, 1947), 339–55; "Adjustment Problems of the Stepchild," *Proc. of the Northwest Annual Conf. on Fam. Rel.* (1948), 87–98; and "The Stepmother," *Sociology and Social Research, 33* (May–June 1949), 342–47.

⁸Jessie Bernard, *Remarriage*, New York: Dryden Press, 1956.

⁹William J. Goode, *Women in Divorce*, New York: Free Press, 1956.

¹⁰Charles E. Bowerman and Donald P. Irish, "Some Relationships of Stepchildren to Their Parents," in Ruth S. Cavan (ed.), *Marriage and Family in the Modern World*, New York: Thomas Y. Crowell, 1969, 580.

¹¹Anne W. Simon, *Stepchild in the Family*, New York: Pocket Books, 1965.

¹²Among these articles and chapters are: Robert R. Bell, *Marriage and Family Interaction*, Illinois: Dorsey Press, 1963, Chap. 16; Leonard Benson, *Fatherhood: A Sociological Perspective*, New York: Random House, 1968, 265–67; Ruth S. Cavan, *The American Family*, New York: Thomas Y. Crowell, 1969, Chap. 19; Morton W. Hunt, *The World of the Formerly Married*, New York: McGraw-Hill, 1966, 266–93; E.E.

LeMasters, *Parents in Modern America: A Sociological Analysis,* Illinois: Dorsey Press, 1970, 172–74; Gerald R. Leslie, *The Family in Social Context,* New York: Oxford Univ. Press, 1967, 644–48; and Helen Thompson, *The Successful Stepparent,* New York: Harper and Row, 1966.

[13]Floyd Manfield Martinson, *Family in Society,* New York: Dodd, Mead & Co., 1971, "About three out of four remarriages involve a divorced person; one out of four involve a widow or widower," 345.

[14]Bernard, op. cit., and Goode, op. cit. are the exceptions.

[15]For example, Joseph B. Perry and Erdwin H. Pfuhl, "Adjustment of Children in Sole and Remarriage Homes," *Marriage and Family Living 25:* 221–4, 1963; Charles E. Bowerman and Donald P. Irish, "Some Relationships of Stepchildren to Their Parents," *Marr. & Fam. Liv.,* May 1962, 113–21; William J. Good, "Family Disorganization," in Robert K. Merton and Robert A. Nisbet (eds.) *Contemporary Social Problems,* New York: Harcourt, Brace, and World, 1966, 479–552; Benjamin Schlesinger, "Remarriage — An Inventory of Findings," *Family Coordinator 17,* Oct. 1968, 248–50.

[16]U.S. Department of Commerce, Bureau of the Census, *Marital Status and Family Status,* March 1970, 2–3.

[17]U.S. Department of Health, Education, and Welfare, *Divorce Statistics Analysis,* Series 21, No. 17, October 1969, 1.

[18]*Time Magazine,* September 8, 1969, 67–68.

[19]Bernard, op. cit., 64.

[20]Charles Horton Cooley, *Social Organization,* Scribner, 1909. This term was first used as a chapter title, "The Primary Social Group," in A.W. Small and G.E. Vincent, *An Introduction to the Study of Society,* 1894.

[21]See, for example, E. Faris, "The Primary Group, Essence and Accident," *Am. J. of Soc. 37,* 1932, 41–50; and A.P. Bates and N. Babchuck, "The Primary Group: A Reappraisal," *Soc. Q., 2,* 1961, 181–91.

[22]S.C. Lee, "The Primary Group as Cooley Defines It," *Soc. Q., 5,* 1964, 23–24.

[23]Kurt H. Wolff, *The Sociology of George Simmel,* Glencoe, Illinois: Free Press, 1950.

[24]Bernard, op. cit., 14.

[25]One interesting and infrequently considered problem is that of inheritance rights. Marvin B. Sussman, Judith N. Cates, and David T. Smith, in *The Family and Inheritance*

(New York: Russell Sage Foundation, 1970), write that the Ohio Statute of Descent and Distribution, for example, provides that "stepchildren inherit only after the possibilities of other relatives are exhausted; that is, distant cousins inherit before a stepchild does" (109).

[26]Bernard, op. cit., Chapters 8 and 9.

[27]Cavan, *The American Family,* op. cit., 450.

Chapter Two

[1]*Newsletter,* 28, Regional Church Planning Office, Cleveland, Ohio, October 1966.

[2]*18 Decennial Census of the United States, 1960 Census of Population, Vol. I,* Part 37, Ohio, U.S. Department of Commerce, Bureau of the Census, Washington, D.C.

[3]Marriage and Divorce Statistics, *Vital Statistics of the United States,* 1959, Section 2, (United States Department of Health, Education, and Welfare, Public Health Service) 7.

[4]There has been a debate among sociologists concerned with stratification. There are those who favor retention of the concept of social class—Rolf Dahrendorf, Gerhard Lenski, and T.B. Bottomore—whose arguments are based generally on the remarks in the body of this chapter. There are also those who believe the concept should be dispensed with— Dennis Wrong in particular—who feel the concept should be replaced with one of inequality. Wrong writes that economic differences are diminishing and therefore emphasis should shift to status differences if differentiation is to be maintained. I feel that the concept is an important one and should be retained.

[5]William J. Goode, *After Divorce,* (Glencoe, Ill.: Free Press, 1956); William M. Kephart, "Occupational Level and Marital Disruption," *ASR, 20,* 1955, 456–65; Thomas P. Monahan, "Divorce by Occupational Level," *Marr. & Fam. Liv., 17,* 1955, 322–24; and H. Ashley Weeks, "Differential Divorce Rates by Occupation," *Social Forces, 21,* 1943, 34–37. It is interesting to note that the divorce rates are lower among the unskilled than the semiskilled. This is usually accounted for by the cost of divorce or religious restrictions against it and is compensated for by the higher rate of separation and desertion.

[6]Robert O. Blood, Jr. and Donald M. Wolfe, *Husbands and Wives* (New York: Free Press, 1960) Chapter 9.

Chapter Three

[1]Ernest W. Burgess, "The Family as a Unity of Interacting Personalities," *The Family, 7,* 1926, 5.

[2]One interesting and unexpected finding was the number of couples in the sample in which the wife was older than the husband. Twenty couples, or nearly 23 percent of the sample, were in this category. Thirteen of the wives were between one and three years older, while seven were between four and eight years older. This finding was surprising because in the majority of American marriages husbands are older than wives. When there is a great difference in age, one usually finds an older man with a young wife. Wives who are older than their husbands are in the vast minority.

It is also to be noted that in only two cases was there a considerable difference in age, with the husband older than the wife by twenty-three years in both cases. Neither of these wives had been married before and both the husbands were fathers of children in their late teens. Both couples had had a child together. The husband of one couple and the wife of the other both commented on the attitudes of strangers toward the difference in their ages. Husband: "The only thing people seem curious about is the difference in our ages." Wife: "I think some people look upon us as being strange, but mostly because of the age difference between my husband and me."

[3]William J. Goode, *Women in Divorce,* (New York: Free Press, 1956).

[4]Lewis M. Terman, *Psychological Factors in Marital Happiness* (New York: McGraw-Hill, 1938); Harvey J. Locke, *Predicting Adjustment in Marriage: A Comparison of a Divorced and a Happily Married Group* (New York: Henry Holt, 1951); Ernest W. Burgess and Paul Wallin, *Engagement and Marriage* (Philadelphia: J.B. Lippincott, 1953); Ernest W. Burgess and Leonard S. Cottrell, Jr., *Predicting Success or Failure in Marriage* (Englewood Cliffs, N.J.: Prentice-Hall, 1939); and Robert O. Blood and Donald M. Wolfe, *Husbands and Wives* (New York: Free Press, 1960), 229.

[5]Goode, op. cit.; William M. Kephart, "Occupational Level and Marital Disruption," *ASR, 20,* 1955, 456–65; Thomas P. Monahan, "Divorce by Occupational Level," *Marr. and Fam. Liv., 17,* 1955, 322–24; H. Ashley Weeks, "Differential Divorce

Rates by Occupations," *Social Forces, 21,* 1943, 34–37.

[6]Blood and Wolfe, op. cit., 256.

[7]Lewis M. Terman, op. cit.; and Burgess and Wallin, op. cit.

[8]Of the fifty-five families in the educational difference category, only fifteen, or 27 percent, were those in which the wife had the higher level of education.

Chapter Four

[1]George Levinger, "Marital Cohesiveness and Dissolution: An Integrative Review," *J. Marr. & Fam., 27,* 1965, 19–28. Reprinted in Marvin B. Sussman (ed.), *Sourcebook in Marriage and the Family,* 3rd ed. (Boston: Houghton-Mifflin, 1968), 424.

[2]Harvey J. Locke, *Predicting Adjustment in Marriage: A Comparison of a Divorced and a Happily Married Group* (New York: Henry Holt & Co., 1951).

[3]Jessie Bernard, *Remarriage* (New York: Dryden Press, 1956).

[4]Robert O. Blood, Jr. and Donald M. Wolfe, *Husbands and Wives* (New York: Free Press, 1960).

[5]Ibid.

[6]William J. Goode, *Women in Divorce* (New York: Free Press, 1956) 335.

[7]Blood and Wolfe, op. cit., 226.

[8]Among these are: Harvey J. Locke, op. cit.; and Judson T. Landis and Mary G. Landis, *Building a Successful Marriage,* 4th ed. (Englewood Cliffs, New Jersey: Prentice-Hall, 1963); "Social and Economic Variations in Marriage, Divorce, and Remarriage" (p-20, #223), *Government Printing Office,* Washington, D.C.

[9]J. Richard Udry, *The Social Context of Marriage* (New York: J.B. Lippincott, 1966) 317–24. Udry has taken issue with this contention. He feels that although the data on age at marriage seem to indicate that youth and marital success do not coincide, there are social and psychological factors which intervene. Udry believes that low marital adjustment rates are related to low educational level and low socioeconomic status, both of which are related to young age at marriage. Therefore, he claims, young marriages are unstable, because those who marry young have the characteristics which lead to unstable marriages at any age.

[10]Bernard, op. cit., 11.

[11]Ruth Shonle Cavan, *The American Family,* 4th ed. (New York: Thomas Y. Crowell, 1969) 435.

[12]Goode, op. cit., 335.

[13]Landis and Landis, op. cit., 216.

[14]For example, Lee G. Burchinal and Loren E. Chancellor, "Survival Rates Among Religiously Homogeneous and Interreligious Marriages," *Social Forces, 41*:4, 1963, 353–62.

[15]Locke, op. cit.

[16]Among many others, Robert R. Bell, *Marriage and Family Interaction,* 3rd ed. (Homewood, Illinois: Dorsey Press, 1971) 519.

[17]Ibid., Chap. 21.

[18]Ibid., 530.

[19]Ibid., 530.

[20]For example, Julius Roth and Robert F. Peck, "Social Class and Social Mobility Factors Related to Marital Adjustment," *ASR, 16,* 1951, 479.

[21]Bert N. Adams and Thomas Weirath, *Readings on the Sociology of the Family* (Chicago: Markham, 1971) 257.

Chapter Five

[1]James Walters and Nick Stinnett, "Parent-Child Relationships: A Decade Review of Research," *J. Marr. & Fam., 33*:1, 1971, 82.

[2]Irene Fast and Albert C. Cain, "The Stepparent Role: Potential for Disturbance in Family Functioning," *Am. J. Orthopsychiatry, 36,* 1966, 485–91.

[3]The role of parent in our society is ambiguous. Several investigators find that both men and women are poorly socialized into the role of parent (Orville G. Brim, Jr., *Education for Child Rearing,* New York: Russell Sage Foundation, 1959). Others have stressed the unreal romanticism attached to the role (E.E. LeMasters, "Parenthood as Crisis," *Marr. & Fam. Liv. 19,* 1957, 352–55). Some investigators have noted the erosion of parental authority without a concomitant decrease of parental responsibility (J.M. Mogey, "A Century of Declining Parental Authority," *Marr. & Fam. Liv. 19,* 1957, 234–39). For a more complete discussion of the status of parents, see E. E. LeMasters, *Parents in Modern America* (Homewood, Illinois: Dorsey Press, 1970), especially Chap. 2 and 4.

[4]Leonard Benson, *Fatherhood* (New York: Random House, 1968) 266.

[5]Charles E. Bowerman and Donald P. Irish, "Some Relationships of Stepchildren to Their Parents," *Marr. & Fam. Liv.*, 24, 1962, 113–21.

[6]The origins and the history of this myth were explored by Janet Pfleger, "The 'Wicked Stepmother' in a Child Guidance Clinic," *Smith Coll. Studies in Social Work*, 17, 1946–1947, 125–26.

[7]William C. Smith, "The Stepchild," *ASR*, 10, 1945, 237–42.

[8]Bowerman and Irish, op. cit., 120.

[9]Margaret Mead, "Anomalies in American Postdivorce Relationship," in Paul Bohannan (ed.), *Divorce and After* (Garden City, New York: Doubleday, 1970) 102.

[10]Bohannan, Ibid., 29–56.

[11]F. Ivan Nye, "Child Adjustment in Broken and in Unhappy Unbroken Homes," *Marr. & Fam. Liv.*, 19, 1957, 356–61.

[12]William J. Goode, *After Divorce* (Glencoe, Illinois: Free Press, 1956) 307–9.

[13]Lee G. Burchinal, "Characteristics of Adolescents from Unbroken, Broken, and Reconstituted Families," *J. Marr. & Fam.*, 26, 1964, 44–50.

[14]Jessie Bernard, *Remarriage* (New York: Dryden Press, 1956) 306–11.

[15]Bowerman and Irish, op, cit., 117.

[16]Bernard, op. cit.; Raymond Illsley and Barbara Thompson, "Women from Broken Homes," *Sociological Review*, 9, 1961, 27–54.

[17]Thomas S. Langer and Stanley T. Michael, *Life Stresses and Mental Health* (New York: Free Press, 1963) 174.

[19]Robert R. Bell, *Marriage and Family Interaction*, 3rd ed. (Homewood, Illinois: Dorsey Press, 1971) 543.

[19]Ibid., 543.

[20]Bernard, op. cit., 216.

[21]Ruth S. Cavan, *The American Family*, 4th ed. (New York: Thomas Y. Crowell, 1969) 473.

[22]Bowerman & Irish, op. cit.

[23]Bowerman and Irish found the same sort of division between preference for very young children or quite adult children over adolescent children. The same would probably be true for primary families.

²⁴In about 90 percent of divorce cases which involve children, custody goes to the mother. The custom is based on the assumption that the mother is better able to care for the children than the father. See Robert R. Bell, *Marriage and Family Interaction*, 3rd ed. (Homewood, Ill.: Dorsey Press, 1971) 506.

²⁵On the other hand, one could say the opposite: When the mother is deprived of her biological children, she may demonstrate a great deal of love and warmth to her step-children in order to "prove" that she is a "real" and competent mother.

²⁶Bell, op. cit., 522.

Chapter Six

¹Donald P. Irish, "Sibling Interaction: A Neglected Aspect in Family Life Research," *Social Forces, 42,* 279–88. Reprinted in Marvin B. Sussman (ed.) *Sourcebook on Marriage and the Family*, 3rd ed. (Boston: Houghton Mifflin, 1968) 293–301.

Among those who have done empirical work on sibling interaction are: M.H. Krout, "Typical Behavior Patterns in 26 Ordinal Positions," *J. of Genetic Psychology,* 55, 1939, 3-30; Paulette Cahn, "Sociometric Experiments on Groups of Siblings," *Sociometry,* 15, 1952, 306-310; Carroll Davis and Marry L. Northway, "Siblings — Rivalry or Relationship?" *Bull. of Inst. of Child Study,* 19, 1957, 10-13; Helen Koch, "The Relation in Young Children Between Characteristics of Their Playmates and Certain Attributes of Their Siblings," *Child Development,* 28, 1957, 175-202; Albert Ellis and Robert M. Beechley, "A Comparison of Child Guidance Clinic Patients Coming from Large, Medium, and Small Families," *J. of Genetic Psychology,* 79, 1951, 131-144.

²R. Pherson, "Bilateral Kin Group as a Structural Type," *Univ. of Manila J. of East Asiatic Studies,* 3, 1954, 199–202.

³Elaine Cumming and David M. Schneider, "Sibling Solidarity: A Property of American Kinship," *Am. Anthro.,* 63, 1961, 498–507.

⁴Clifford Kirkpatrick, *The Family as Process and Institution* (New York: Ronald Press, 1963) 247–53.

⁵Ibid., 248–49.

[6]George C. Homans, *The Human Group* (New York: Harcourt Brace, 1950) 111.

Chapter Seven

[1]Elizabeth Bott, *Family and Social Network* (London: Tavistock, 1957).

[2]Jessie Bernard, *Remarriage* (New York: Dryden Press, 1956) 199-207.

[3]William J. Goode, *Women in Divorce* (New York: Free Press, 1956), 301.

[4]Ibid., 211.

[5]David M. Schneider, *American Kinship: A Cultural Account* (Englewood Cliffs, N.J.: Prentice-Hall, 1968).

[6]August B. Hollingshead, "Cultural Factors in the Selection of Marriage Mates," *ASR, 15,* 1950, 619-27.

[7]Leonard Benson, *The Family Bond* (New York: Random House, 1971) 128.

[8]Ibid.

[9]Gerhard Lenski, *The Religious Factor* (New York: Doubleday, 1961) 48-49.

Chapter Eight

[1]Willard Waller, *The Family: A Dynamic Interpretation* (New York: Gordon Co., 1938) 13.

[2]Marvin B. Sussman (ed.) *Sourcebook in Marriage and the Family,* 3rd ed. (Boston: Houghton Mifflin, 1968) 36.

[3]Jeffrey K. Hadden and Marie L. Borgatta, "The American Ideal of Marriage" in Jeffrey Hadden and Marie L. Borgatta (eds.) *Marriage and the Family* (Itasca, Ill.: Peacock Publs., 1969) 220-22.

[4]Norman W. Bell and Ezra F. Vogel, "Toward a Framework for Functional Analysis of Family Behavior" in Norman Bell and Ezra F. Vogel (eds.) *A Modern Introduction to the Family* (Glencoe, Ill.: Free Press, 1960) 1.

[5]Jesse R. Pitts, "The Structural-Functional Approach," in Harold T. Christensen (ed.), *Handbook on Marriage and the Family,* (Chicago: Rand McNally, 1964) 56.

[6]Leonard Benson, *The Family Bond* (New York: Random House, 1971) 9-11.

[7]Ibid., 11-13.

[8]Donald P. Irish, "Sibling Interaction: A Neglected Aspect in Family Life Research," *Social Forces 42,* 1964, 279-88.

[9]Lippitt was able to show that older siblings can often

socalize younger brothers and sisters more efficiently than parents. Ronald Lippitt, "Improving the Socialization Process" in John A. Clausen (ed.) *Socialization and Society* (Boston: Little, Brown, 1968) 321–74.

[10]Reuben Hill and Joan Aldous, "Socialization for Marriage and Parenthood" in David A. Goslin (ed.) *Handbook of Socialization Theory and Research* (Chicago: Rand McNally, 1969) 906.

[11]Ibid., 906.

[12]*Statistical Abstracts of the United States,* 1967 (Washington, D.C.: Government Printing Office, 1967) 64.

[13]Ronald Freedman, Pascal K. Whelpton, and Arthur A. Campbell, *Family Planning, Sterility, and Population Growth* (New York: McGraw-Hill, 1959) 216–26. Ninety-four per cent of the 2700 women in this national probability sample considered two to four children ideal.

[14]*Statistical Abstracts of the United States,* 1961 (Washington, D.C.: Government Printing Office, 1961) 53.

[15]*Stat. Abs.,* 1967, op. cit. Mean age at time of marriage varies directly with social class.

[16]Paul H. Besancency, *Interfaith Marriage* (New Haven, Conn.: College and University Press, 1970) 54–55.

[17]Larry D. Barnett, "Interracial Marriage in California," *Marr. & Fam. Liv., 25,* 1963, 424–27.

[18]Ruby Jo Kennedy, "Single or Triple Melting Pot?" Intermarriage Trends in New Haven 1910-1940," *AJS, 49,* 1944, 333.

[19]Zick Rubin, "Do American Women Marry Up?" *ASR, 33,* 1968, 750–60.

[20]Christensen, op. cit., 234-35.

[21]Ruth S. Cavan, *The American Family,* 4th ed. (New York: Thomas Y. Crowell, 1969) 332.

[22]Robert R. Blood, Jr. and Donald M. Wolfe, *Husbands and Wives* (New York: Free Press, 1960) Chap. 6.

[23]Ibid., 223.

[24]Jetse Sprey, "Are Most People Dissatisfied with Their Sexual Life?" *Sexual Behavior,* December 1971, 52–53.

[25]Christensen, op. cit., Chap. 12.

[26]Blood and Wolfe, op. cit., 73.

[27]Blood and Wolfe, op. cit., 134–35; Ernest W. Burgess and Paul Waller, *Engagement and Marriage* (Chicago: J.B. Lippincott, 1953) 707.

[28]Robert Bell, op. cit., 452.

[29]Christensen and Johnsen, op. cit., 434.

[30]Robert Bell, op. cit., 467–73.

[31]Irish, op. cit.

[32]Marvin B. Sussman and Lee Burchinal, "Kin Family Network: Unheralded Structures in Current Conceptualizations of Family Functioning," in Marvin B. Sussman (ed.) *Sourcebook in Marriage and the Family,* 3rd ed. (Boston: Houghton Mifflin, 1968) 72.

[33]Marvin B. Sussman, "The Isolated Nuclear Family: Fact or Fiction?" Sussman, Ibid., 94.

Bibliography

Adams, Bert N., and Thomas Weirath. *Readings on the Sociology of the Family.* Chicago: Markham, 1971.

Barnett, Larry D. "Interracial Marriage in California." *Marriage and Family Living* 25:424–27, 1963.

Bates, A.P., and N. Babchuck. "The Primary Group: A Reappraisal." *Sociological Quarterly* 2:181–91, 1961

Bell, Norman W., and Ezra F. Vogel. "Toward a Framework for Functional Analysis of Family Behavior." In *A Modern Introduction to the Family*, edited by Norman W. Bell and Ezra F. Vogel. Glencoe, Illinois: Free Press, 1960.

Bell, Robert R. *Marriage and Family Interaction.* Illinois: Dorsey, 1963.

Benson, Leonard. *Fatherhood: A Sociological Perspective.* New York: Random House, 1968.

Bernard, Jessie. *Remarriage.* New York: Dryden Press, 1956.

Besancency, Paul H. *Interfaith Marriages*. New Haven, Connecticut: College and University Press, 1970.

Blood, Robert O., Jr., and Donald M. Wolfe. *Husbands and Wives*. New York: Free Press, 1960.

Bott, Elizabeth. *Family and Social Network*. London: Tavistock, 1957.

Bowerman, Charles E., and Donald P. Irish. "Some Relationships of Stepchildren to Their Parents." In *Marriage and Family in the Modern World*, edited by Ruth Shonle Cavan. New York: Thomas Y. Crowell, 1969.

Burchinal, Lee G. "Characteristics of Adolescents from Unbroken, Broken, and Reconstituted Families." *Journal of Marriage and the Family* 26:44—50, 1964.

———. and Loren E. Chancellor. "Survival Rates Among Religiously Homogeneous and Interreligious Marriages." *Social Forces* 41:353–62, 1963.

———. William F. Kenkel, and Loren E. Chancellor. "Comparison of State and Diocese-Reported Marriage Data for Iowa." *American Catholic Sociological Review* 23:21-29, 1962.

Burgess, Ernest W. "The Family as a Unity of Interacting Personalities." *The Family* 7:5, 1926.

———. and Leonard S. Cottrell, Jr. *Predicting Success or Failure in Marriage*. Englewood Cliffs, New Jersey: Prentice-Hall, 1939.

———. and Paul Wallin. *Engagement and Marriage*. Philadelphia: Lippincott, 1953.

Cavan, Ruth Shonle. *The American Family*, 4th ed. New York: Thomas Y. Crowell, 1969.

Cahn, Paulette. "Sociometric Experiments on Groups of Siblings." *Sociometry* 15:306–10, 1952.

Chen, Ronald. "The Dilemma of Divorce: Disaster or Remedy?" *Family Coordinator* 17:252, 1968.

Cogswell, Betty E., and Marvin B. Sussman. "Changing Family and Marriage Forms: Complications for Human Service Systems." *Family Coordinator*, 21:4, 505–16, 1972.

Cooley, Charles Horton. *Social Organization*. Scribner, 1909.

Cumming, Elaine, and David M. Schneider. "Sibling

Solidarity: A Property of American Kinship." *American Anthropologist* 63:498–507, 1961.

Davis, Carroll, and Marry L. Northway. "Siblings—Rivalry or Relationship?" *Bulletin of the Institute of Child Study* 19:10–13, 1957.

Deutsch, Helene. *The Psychology of Women.* New York: Grune & Stratton, 1944.

Ellis, Albert, and Robert M. Beechley. "A Comparison of Child Guidance Clinic Patients Coming from Large, Medium, and Small Families." *Journal of Genetic Psychology* 79:131–44, 1951.

Faris, E., "The Primary Group: Essence and Accident." *American Journal of Sociology* 37:41–50, 1932.

Fast, Irene, and Albert C. Cain. "The Stepparent Role: Potential for Distrubance in Family Functioning." *American Journal of Orthopsychiatry* 36:485–91, 1966.

Fortes, M. "Step-parenthood and Juvenile Delinquency," *Sociological Review* 25:153–58, 1933.

Freedman, Ronald, Rascal K. Whelpton, and Arthur A. Cambell. *Family Planning, Sterility, and Population Growth.* New York: McGraw-Hill, 1959.

Fuller, Richard C., and Richard R. Myers. "The Natural History of a Social Problem." *American Sociological Review* 6:320, 1941.

Garfinkel, Harold. *Studies in Ethnomethodology.* Englewood Cliffs, New Jersey: Prentice-Hall, 1967.

Goode, William J. *Women in Divorce.* New York: Free Press, 1956.

———. "Family Disorganization." In *Contemporary Social Problems,* edited by Robert K. Merton and Robert A. Nisbet, pp. 479–552. New York: Harcourt Brace & World, 1966.

Hadden, Jeffrey K., and Marie L. Borgatta. "The American Ideal of Marriage." In *Marriage and the Family,* edited by Jeffrey K. Hadden and Marie L. Borgatta, pp. 220–22. Itasca, Illinois: Peacock, 1969.

Heilpern, Else P. "Psychological Problems of Step-children." *Psychological Review* 30:163–76, 1943.

Hill, Reuben, and Joan Aldous. "Socialization for Marriage and Parenthood." In *Handbook of Socialization Theory and Research,* edited by David A. Coslin. Chicago: Rand McNally, 1969.

Hoenig, C. "Die Stiefalternfamilie des Stiefkindes." *Zeitschrift für Kinderforschuno* 24:188–331, 1928.

Hollingshead, August B. "Cultural Factors in the Selection of Marriage Mates." *American Sociological Review* 15:619–27, 1950.

Homans, George C. *The Human Group.* New York: Harcourt, Brace, 1950.

Hunt, Morton W. *The World of the Formerly Married.* New York: McGraw-Hill, 1966.

Illsley, Raymond, and Barbara Thompson. "Women From Broken Homes." *Sociological Review* 9:27–54, 1961.

Irish, Donald P. "Sibling Interaction: A Neglected Aspect in Family Life Research." *Social Forces* 42:279–88.

Kennedy, Ruby Jo. "Single or Triple Melting Pot?" *American Journal of Sociology* 49:333, 1944.

Kephart, William M. "Occupational Level and Marital Disruption," *American Sociological Review* 20, 456–65, 1955.

———.*The Family, Society, and the Individual,* 2nd ed. Boston: Houghton Mifflin, 1966.

Kirkpatrick, Clifford. *The Family as Process and Institution.* 2nd ed. New York: Ronald Press, 1963.

Koch, Helen. "The Relation in Young Children Between Characteristics of Their Playmates and Certain Attributes of Their Siblings." *Child Development* 28:175–202, 1957.

Krout, M.H. "Typical Behavior Patterns in 26 Ordinal Positions." *Journal of Genetic Psychology* 55:3–30, 1939.

Kuhn, Hannah. "Psychologische Untersuchungen Uber das Stiefmutter-problem: Die Konfliktmoglichkeiten in der Stiefmutter-familie and ihre Bedeutung für die Verwahrlosung des Stiefkinds." *Zeitschrift für angewandte Psychologie* 45:1–185, 1929.

Landecker, Werner S. "Types of Integration and Their

Measurement." *American Journal of Sociology* LVI:332–40, 1951.

Landis, Judson T., and Mary G. Landis. *Building a Successful Marriage.* 4th ed. Englewood Cliffs, New Jersey: Prentice-Hall, 1963.

Langner, Thomas S., and Stanley T. Michael. *Life Stresses and Mental Health.* New York: Free Press, 1963.

Lee, S.C. "The Primary Group as Cooley Defines It." *Sociological Quarterly* 5:23–34, 1964.

Lenski, Gerhard. *The Religious Factor.* New York: Doubleday, 1961.

Leslie, Gerald R. *The Family in Social Context.* New York: Oxford University Press, 1956.

Levinger, George. "Marital Cohesiveness and Dissolution: An Integrative Review." *Journal of Marriage and the Family* 27:19–28, 1965.

Lippitt, Ronald. "Improving the Socialization Process." In *Socialization and Society,* edited by Joan A. Clausen, pp. 321–74. Boston: Little, Brown, 1968.

Locke, Harvey J. *Predicting Adjustment in Marriage: A Comparison of a Divorced and a Happily Married Group.* New York: Henry Holt, 1951.

Martinson, Floyd Mansfield. *Family in Society.* New York: Dodd, Mead, 1971.

Mead, Margaret. "Anomalies in American Postdivorce Relationships." In *Divorce and After,* edited by Paul Bohannan. Garden City, New York: Doubleday, 1970.

Meriam, Adele Stuart. *The Stepfather in the Family.* Chicago: University of Chicago Press, 1940.

———. "Stepfather in the Family." *Social Service Review* 14, 655–77, 1940.

Miller, Delbert C. *Handbook of Research Design and Social Measurement.* New York: David McKay, 1964.

Monahan, Thomas P. "Divorce by Occupational Level." *Marriage and Family Living* 17:322–24, 1955.

Mudroch, R. "Das Stiefkind." *Versammlung für Kinderforschung* 4:216–28, 1932.

Natenson, Maurice. *Philosophy of the Social Sciences.*

New York: Random House, 1963.

Neuman, G. "Untersuchungen uber das Verhaltnis Zwischen Stiefmutter und Stiefkind." *Zeitschrift für Padagogische Psychologie* 34:348–67, 1933.

Nye, Ivan, and William Rushing. "Toward Family Measurement Research." In *Marriage and the Family,* edited by Jeffrey K. Hadden and Marie L. Borgatta, pp. 133–40. Illinois: Peacock Press, 1969.

Perry, Joseph, and Erdwin H. Pfuhl. "Adjustment of Children in Sole and Remarriage Homes." *Marriage and Family Living* 25, 221–24, 1963.

Pfleger, Janet. "The 'Wicked Stepmother' in a Child Guidance Clinic." *Smith College Studies in Social Work* 17:125–26, 1946.

Pherson, R. "Bilateral Kin Group as a Structural Type." *Univ. of Manila Journal of East Asiatic Studies* 3:199–202, 1954.

Pitts, Jesse R. "The Structural-Functional Approach." In *Handbook of Marriage and the Family,* edited by Harold T. Christensen, Chicago: Rand McNally, p. 56, 1964.

Roe, Anne, and Marvin Seigelman. "A Parent–Child Relations Questionnaire." *Child Development* 34: 355–69, 1963.

Rogers, Everett M., and Hans Sebald. "Familism, Family Integration, and Kinship Orientation." *Marriage and Family Living* 24:25–30, 1962.

Rosenberg, Morris. "Parental Interest and Children's Self Conceptions." *Sociometry* 26:35–49, 1963.

Rosenthal, Erich. "Studies of Jewish Intermarriage in the United States." *American Jewish Year Book* 64:39, 1963.

Roth, Julius, and Robert F. Pack. "Social Class and Social Mobility Factors Related to Marital Adjustment." *American Sociological Review* 16:479, 1951.

Rubin, Zick. "Do American Women Marry Up?" *American Sociological Review* 33:750–60, 1968.

Ruhler, Alice. "Das Stiefkin." *Schwerezichbare Kinder,* 1927.

Schneider, David M. *American Kinship: A Cultural Account.* Englewood Cliffs, New Jersey: Prentice-Hall, 1968.

Schlesinger, Benjamin. "Remarriage—An Inventory of Findings." *Family Coordinator* 17, 248–50, 1968.

Sebald, Hans, and Wade H. Andrew. "Family Integration and Related Factors in a Rural Fringe Population." *Marriage and Family Living* 24:347–51, 1962.

Shils, Edward A. "The Study of the Primary Group." In *The Policy Sciences—Recent Developments in Scope and Methods,* edited by Daniel Lerner and Harold D. Lasswell. Palo Alto: Stanford University Press, 1951.

Simon, Anne W. *Stepchild in the Family.* New York: Pocketbooks, 1965.

Small, A.W., and G.E. Vincent. *An Introduction to the Study of Society.* 1894.

Smith, William C. "The Stepchild." *American Sociological Review* 10:237–42, 1945.

——."Remarriage and the Stepchild." In *Successful Marriage,* edited by Morris Fishbein and Ernest W. Burgess, pp. 339–55. New York: Doubleday, 1947.

——."Adjustment Problems of the Stepchild." *Proceedings of the Northwest Annual Conference on Family Relations.* 1948.

——. "The Stepmother." *Sociology and Social Research* 33:342–47, 1949.

——. *The Stepchild.* Chicago: University of Chicago Press, 1953.

Sprey, Jetse. "Are Most People Dissatisfied with Their Sexual Life?" *Sexual Behavior,* December, 1971.

Stern, Erich. "Beitrag zur Psychologie des Stiefkindes." *Zeitschrift für Kinderforschung* 24:144–57, 1928.

Sussman, Marvin B. "Changing Families in a Changing Society: Report of Forum 14." In *Report to the President: 1970 White House Conference on Children.* Washington, D.C., Government Printing Office, 1971.

——."Family Systems in the 1970's: Analysis, Politics, Programs." *Annals of American Academy of*

Political and Social Science, 396, 40–56, 1971.

———. "A Family Policy." Mimeographed. Groves Conference of Marriage and the Family, Winston-Salem, North Carolina, 1970.

———. "The Isolated Nuclear Family: Fact or Fiction?" In *Sourcebook of Marriage and the Family,* edited by Marvin B. Sussman. Chicago: Rand McNally, 1968.

———, and Lee Burchinal. "Kin Family Network: Unheralded Structures in Current Conceptualization of Family Functioning." In *Handbook of Marriage and the Family,* edited by Marvin Sussman. Chicago: Rand McNally, 1968.

———, and Betty E. Cogswell. "The Meaning of Variant and Experimental Marriage Styles and Family Forms in the 1970's." *The Family Coordinator* 21:4, 1972.

Swanson, G.E. "To Live in Concord With a Society: Two Empirical Studies of Primary Relations." In *Cooley and Sociological Analysis,* edited by A.J. Reiss, p. 87. Ann Arbor: University of Michigan Press, 1968.

Terman, Lewis M. *Psychological Factors in Marital Happiness.* New York: McGraw-Hill, 1938.

Time Magazine, September 8, 1969, pp. 67–68.

Thomson, Helen. *The Successful Stepparent.* New York: Harper & Row, 1966.

United States, Dept. of Health, Education & Welfare. *Divorce Statistics Analysis,* series 21, number 17, 1967.

United States, Dept. of Commerce, Bureau of Census. *Marital Status & Family Status.* Washington, D.C.: Government Printing Office, 1970, pp. 2–3.

United States, Dept. of Commerce, Bureau of the Census. *Census of Population 1960,* vol. 1. 18th Decennial Census of the United States, part 37, Ohio. Washington, D.C.: Government Printing Office, 1960.

United States, Dept. of Health, Education & Welfare. *Marriage and Divorce Statistics, Vital Statistics of the United States,* section 2. Washington, D.C.: Government Printing Office, 1969.

United States, Dept. of Health, Education & Welfare. "Social and Economic Variations in Marriage, Divorce, and Remarriage." Number 223. Washington, D.C.: Government Printing Office, 1959.

United States Statistical Abstracts. Dept. of Commerce, Bureau of the Census. Washington, D.C.: Government Printing Office, 1961 and 1967.

Von Lincke, Werner. "Das Stiefmuttermotiv in Marchen der Germanischen Volker." *Germanische Studien* 142, 1933.

Waller, Willard. *The Family: A Dynamic Interpretation.* New York: Gordon, 1938.

Walters, James, and Nick Stinnett. "Parent-Child Relationships: A Decade Review of Research." *Journal of Marriage and the Family* 33:82, 1971.

Weeks, H. Ashley. "Differential Divorce Rates by Occupation." *Social Forces* 21:34–37, 1943.

White, Anne M. "Factors Making for Difficulty in the Step-parent Relationship with Children." *Smith College Studies in Social Work* 14:242, 1943.

Wittels, Fritz. Die Befrieung des Kindes. *Hippokrates Verlag.* 4th ed. 1927.

Index

About the author

Lucile Duberman, a sociologist, is an assistant professor at Rutgers University. She has also taught at Brooklyn College.

Educated at Brooklyn College, New York University and Case Western Reserve University, Professor Duberman's main interests are the sociology of marriage and the family and the sociology of sex roles. She has written several books on these themes, as well as articles which have appeared in *Journal of Marriage and the Family, Contemporary Sociology,* and *International Mental Health Newsletter.*

Dr. Duberman is a member of the American Sociological Association, Eastern Sociological Society, National Council on Family Relations, Society for the Study of Social Problems, Sociologists for Women in Society, Society for the Psychological Study of Social Issues, and the National Organization for Women.